Fast Facts on Islam

John Ankerberg
and John Weldon

HARVEST HOUSE PUBLISHERS
Eugene, Oregon 97402

Cover by Terry Dugan Design, Minneapolis, Minnesota

FAST FACTS ON ISLAM
Copyright © 2001 by John Ankerberg and John Weldon
Published by Harvest House Publishers
Eugene, Oregon 97402

Library of Congress Cataloging-in-Publication Data
Ankerberg, John, 1945-
    Fast facts on Islam / John Ankerberg and John Weldon
        p. cm.
    Includes bibliographical references.
    ISBN 0-7369-1011-5 (pbk.)
    1. Islam—Controversial literature. I. Title: Fast facts on Islam. II. Weldon, John. III. Title
    BT1170 .A553 2002
    297—dc21   2001006350

01 02 03 04 05 06 07 08 09 10 / BC-MS / 10 9 8 7 6 5 4 3 2 1

For the innocent,
for the brave,
for those who stay the course.

ACKNOWLEDGMENTS

I (Weldon) owe much of my inspiration for this book to the noble example of the passengers of American Airlines Flight 93, whose bravery and sacrifice prevented the death of many others and the destruction of our nation's seat of government.

"We almost lost the Capitol of the United States."
—Senator Robert Torricelli, September 12, 2001, on CNN

CONTENTS

SECTION V
THE CONNECTION BETWEEN ISLAM AND TERRORISM

ISLAM—NEW QUESTIONS FOR A NEW TIME

Who can forget the day that changed America?

Things changed for everyone on September 11, 2001: Terrorism and radical Islam bloodied American soil in a way that will never be forgotten. A nation's peace became a river of tears.

Consider a few of the facts that no American history book will ignore:

- On our own soil, Americans experienced the worst terrorist attack in human history. "It looked like the entrance to hell" was the common response of rescue workers and authorized visitors to the site of the destruction in New York City. Their repeated comment was that TV news pictures were utterly unable to convey the horror spread in front of them.

- The volatile world of Islam was thrown into an internal crisis that will last for years and that presents an uncertain outcome. One young Muslim woman interviewed by a CBS reporter said, "I want to take back my religion from people who preach hatred. My religion is not about hatred." The news segment concluded sadly by noting that Muslims would have to learn how hard it is to live in an America where now "Islam is equated with terror."

- Tens of millions of Americans no longer felt safe—either in the air or on the ground. Even months after the attack, millions were still afraid, even terrified.

- Americans discovered that a lot of Muslims, especially Arab Muslims, really don't like us much. In fact, many of them hate us. Americans couldn't fathom how the problems of others—for which they had no responsibility, moral or otherwise—required strangers to hate us or kill us.
- A "holy war" was declared on America by the Taliban of Afghanistan, a radical Islamic sect.
- Americans realized that the terrorists had dealt not just the United States, but the entire global economy a blow—setting it back by an estimated $160 billion, according to one analyst. The attack of September 11 thus became an attack upon the world itself.

Americans wanted answers. What motivated people to do such terrifically evil things? Why do so many Muslims hate the U.S.? What is this talk of a heavenly Paradise being guaranteed to murderers who kill innocent people? What exactly does the religion of Islam believe in, and how did it begin? What do the 2 million Muslims living in America believe? In particular, what does Islam believe about *jihad,* or "holy war," and was this related to the horror of September 11? Why do Muslims around the world, and even in America, have such a seemingly irrational hatred for Israel, a democracy that actively supports Western values and moral sensibilities?

In this book we will supply the answers to these important questions—and more. As Americans, we must seek to understand one of the world's great religious, political, and spiritual forces. And as Christians, we must come to comprehend the power of Islam in light of the far greater power that lies within us—the power of God through Jesus Christ.

WHY THESE QUESTIONS
ABOUT ISLAM ARE SO URGENT TODAY

Great harm has been done to us....I will not forget
this wound to our country or those who inflicted it.

> I will not yield; I will not rest; I will not relent in
> waging this struggle for freedom and security for
> the American people.. .The course of this conflict
> is not known, yet its outcome is certain. Freedom
> and fear, justice and cruelty, have always been at
> war, and we know that God is not neutral between
> them....
>
> —President George W. Bush, in his historic address to the
> U.S. Congress and the nation, September 20, 2001

The breadth and scope of the tragedy of September 11 had been unimaginable just a day before. When more than 5,000 people died in the worst terrorist attack in U.S. history, the toll surpassed the casualties of the entire American Revolution; of the Civil War battle of Antietam; of Pearl Harbor—even of D-day. Thousands of children lost parents. The nation quickly crossed the threshold into a state of shock.

Terrorism, of course, was new to no one. From 1981 through 2000, there had been more than 9,000 terrorist attacks worldwide (excluding violence in Palestine), an average of 460 attacks per year.[1]

But in its treachery and savageness, nothing like this, ever. From 1995 through 2000, only 77 Americans had died as a result of international terrorist attacks—an average of 13 deaths per year.[2] On September 11, Americans saw more than 5,000 deaths in just a few hours—a seventyfold increase. (And only the time interval between the impacts on the Trade Towers and the towers' collapse prevented a far greater toll.)

On September 23, 2001, less than two weeks after the attack, Secretary of Defense Donald Rumsfeld was asked by reporters for CNN, "How will we know when we have won the war?" His response: "'Victory in the war' will be when we can do exactly what we did on September tenth." He spoke of normal things, like walking outside the house and not fearing a terrorist attack.

That shows how big a blow the terrorists had dealt us.

America, indeed the civilized world, was outraged, and rightly so. Few understood what could ever motivate people to commit such acts of unparalleled barbarism. Words failed everyone. But America responded with incredible generosity to the victims, and with a resolve for justice that would lead us into a new war.

The European Union gathered in emergency summit to support the U.S. in its war against terrorism. All 34 members of the Organization of American States stood with America. For the first time in history, NATO invoked and implemented Article 5 of its charter: "An attack upon one is an attack upon all."[3]

America had begun the largest offensive and defensive military operation since World War II.

What and Why?

But a very important question remained to be answered—just what had happened, and why?

What had happened was this: America had been rudely awakened to a festering hostility that had been growing around the world for more than a generation. Today, that hostility has been superheated by a radical form of Islam existing in a loose-knit but powerful network spanning the globe, a network that is even supported by various nation–states, such as Iran, Syria, and Iraq. This "Islamism" not only has social, economic, and political goals, but far more ambitious religious goals as well. This radical Islam sees the world as existing in two divisions and no others—the world of faith in Allah *(dar al-Islam)* and the world of unbelief, or faith in false gods— polytheism, trinitarianism, materialism, or anything else that does not conform to Islamic law, or *sharia*. This other division is designated as *dar al-harb,* literally, the "abode of war" (and sometimes termed *dar al-kufr,* or the "abode of apostasy").

For this kind of Islam, the world and all it contains are destined to become the permanent abode of Allah, and any and all means are justified in achieving this end. One of its particularly heinous teachings is that murdering innocent civilians will guarantee zealots residence in a heavenly paradise forever. In fact, bravely dying as a "martyr for Islam" offers the *only* guarantee of paradise that is available in this life. For these radicals, no one outside Islam is innocent, not even, potentially, other Muslims.

Here is a new enemy whose ice-cold stare and bloodstained hands have irrevocably changed the way Americans look at their future, and very likely even the way the entire world will think and operate from now on.

Before we further consider this new future and the new conflict it has brought us into, we need to take a searching and honest look at the religion of Islam—its history, its beliefs, its Bible, and its religious teachings. This will then help us to determine in what ways Islam is and isn't involved in the current critical world events and the struggle against terrorism.

No less an authority than Dr. Daniel Pipes of the Middle East Forum has stated that fully 50 percent of the Muslim world is against the U.S. and would sympathize with Osama bin Laden.[4] Only if we understand what Islam is and what it isn't, and how it is or isn't involved, can we understand what is happening in our world. Indeed, no one anywhere should be unwilling to learn about this important religion, since the fate of the West just might be intertwined with the eventual fate of Islam.

THE RELIGION OF ISLAM: INTRODUCTION

WHAT IS ISLAM?

Islam is the world religion founded by an Arabian visionary named Muhammad (lived from about 570 to 632 A.D.; variant spellings: Muhammed, Mohammed), who was born in the city of Mecca in Arabia. Muhammad claimed he received supernatural revelations from God through the angel Gabriel. These revelations were written down by others and compiled into a book called the Quran, the Muslim Bible (variant spelling: Koran).

Muslims today are divided into *Sunnis* (about 90 percent) and *Shiites* (about 10 percent), as well as millions of Muslim mystics called *Sufis*. In America, Muslim influence is seen both in traditional Islam and in the black Muslim movement.[5] There are now about 2 million Muslims in America, and their numbers are continuing to expand. (In 1990 there were some 30 *mosques*—Muslim houses of worship—in the U.S.; by 2001, there were more than 3,000. See information about two new studies of the U.S. Muslim population at Middle East Forum, <http://www.meforum.org/articles/article.php?id=76>.)

More than any other single factor, the followers of Islam have their lives directed by the book they believe is the Word of God—the Quran. Dr. J. Christy Wilson of Princeton University comments, "Next to the Bible, it is the most esteemed and most powerful book in the world."[6] Whatever Muslims believe and do, it is the teachings in the Quran that have inspired these beliefs and actions. This is why no one should underestimate the importance of this holy book.

Muslims may refuse to approve translations of the Quran, but since 90 percent of Muslims around the world do not know Arabic and *must* use a translation, the point seems to be moot. A good English translation does generally provide sufficiently accurate meanings of the original. (The reader should understand that translations of the Quran may vary at places. Where we have merely cited a verse reference and not the translation it came from, the reader may have to check all translations cited to find that particular wording.)[7]

WHY IS ISLAM IMPORTANT?

Islam is important because it has the power to change the destinies of hundreds of millions of people—and perhaps of the West itself. Consider these points.

- There are 1.3 billion followers of Islam in the world.
- The collective power of Islam is able to dramatically influence the world economy through the Organization of the Petroleum Exporting Countries (OPEC).
- The growing religious influence of Islam outside Islamic nations is unmistakable.
- Islam has the ability to play a key role in the social stability or instability of dozens of governments around the world.
- A principal goal of Islam is to bring Islamic law to every nation.[8]

• Arab nationalism and the Muslim religion have become the single most crucial issue in the volatile Middle East, now a focal point for the attention of the entire world. No one can know how a major crisis in that region may ultimately affect the rest of the world, but the possibilities are sobering.[9]

Islam may be the fastest-growing religion in the world; it is a driving force behind some 50 nations in the Middle East, Africa, and Asia. Indeed, some 35 countries now have populations that are at least 87 percent Muslim. Islam is now the second-largest religion in Europe and the third-largest in the U.S.

The ideological influence of Islam expands to other nations on a daily basis, and Islamic fundamentalism is increasingly aggressive, as the attacks of September 2001 indicated. Religiously, socially, politically, economically, and militarily, Islam will continue to powerfully impact our world.

3

How Did Islam Begin?

Islam began with the supernatural visions and revelations that Muhammad claimed he received from God through the angel Gabriel beginning in 610 A.D. Because Muhammad was uneducated and could neither read nor write, these revelations were first memorized and then later written down by his followers. The authoritative *Cambridge History of Islam* discusses these revelations by noting that "either in the course of the visions or shortly afterwards, Muhammad began to receive 'messages' or 'revelations' from God....He believed that he could easily distinguish between his own thinking and these revelations....Muhammad continued to receive the messages at intervals until his death."[10]

Whatever Islam has accomplished historically, whatever it is today, it results largely from these revelations received by Muhammad some 1,400 years ago.

However, at the end of his life, Muhammad failed to name a successor. This failure resulted in the major division of Islam into the majority Sunni and minority Shiite branches, each claiming to be true Islam. These divisions disagree as to the legitimate successor of Muhammad and over who offers the most accurate representation of Islamic faith.[11]

WHAT ARE THE BASIC MUSLIM BELIEFS?

Muslims must accept six basic beliefs, or articles, of Islamic faith. They are—

- *Faith in Allah.* Muslims believe there is only one true God and that his name is Allah. His will is supreme.

- *Angels.* Muslims believe in angels—such as "Gabriel," who allegedly transmitted the Quran to Muhammad.

- *The Holy Books.* Muslims believe that Allah has given a long series of revelations, including the Old and New Testaments. But these revelations end with the Quran, which supersedes and essentially abrogates the others. (Questions 11–15 and 16–19 deal with the Quran in more detail.)

- *The Prophets.* Muslims believe Allah has sent numerous prophets to mankind. Six of the principal prophets are Adam, the chosen of Allah; Noah, the preacher of Allah; Abraham, the friend of Allah; Moses, the speaker of Allah; Jesus, the word of Allah; and Muhammad, the apostle of Allah.

  Because Muhammad's revelation is considered the greatest of all, he is called the "Seal of the Prophets" and "Peace of the World," among the more than 200 appellations given him.

- *Predestination.* Muslims believe that everything that happens, both good and evil, is predestined by Allah's will, which is his immutable decree.

- *The Day of Judgment.* Muslims believe that on this day the good and evil deeds of all people will be placed on a "scale." Those Muslims having sufficient personal merit and righteousness (and the requisite favor of Allah) will go to eternal heaven; all others will go to eternal hell.

These required articles of faith are also related to specific Muslim practices.

WHAT RELIGIOUS DUTIES ARE REQUIRED OF ALL MUSLIMS?

Every Muslim must practice at least five fundamental religious duties. These are known as the "Pillars of Religion." They are considered obligatory observances upon which the Muslim faith rests.

1. *Reciting the creed of Islam*—"There is no God but Allah and Muhammad is his prophet."

2. *Prayer.* Muslims must recite prescribed prayers five times a day. Each time they must adopt a physical posture: standing, kneeling, hands and face to the ground, and so on. The call to prayer is sounded by a Muslim *muezzin* (crier) from a tower called a *minaret.* This is part of the Muslim church or public place of worship called the *mosque.*

3. *Observing the month of fasting called Ramadan.* This fast commemorates the first revelation of the Quran that Mohammad received in 610 A.D. Although eating is permitted at night, for an entire month Muslims must fast during the day.

4. *Giving alms to the poor.* Muslims are required to give 2½ percent of their currency plus other forms of wealth, as determined by a complicated system.

5. *Pilgrimage to Mecca,* Muhammad's place of birth. This is required at least once during the lifetime of every Muslim who is physically and financially able to make the trip (unless he or she is a slave).

6. *Jihad,* often translated "holy war." *Jihad* is often associated with the above five pillars. It may be interpreted as internal (as spiritual struggle) or external (defending Islam). When the situation

warrants it, this duty requires Muslims to go to war to defend Islam against its perceived enemies. Anyone who dies bravely in a holy war is guaranteed eternal life in Paradise and is considered a martyr for Islam. (See questions 21–23 and 31 for more discussion of *jihad*.) Depending on how it is defined, Muslims may consider *Jihad* obligatory.

How Does Islam View the U.S. and Israel?

Millions of Muslims, even Arab Muslims, do not hate America; in fact, they respect and envy America. (Indeed, this is often true of terrorist radicals themselves, as we will later see.)

However, this is not the case with Israel. At best, there is a strong resentment of that nation. This is because of what many Arab Muslims teach about the land of Palestine—that Allah has decreed it to the Muslims. Large numbers even of moderate Arab Muslims see Israel as a thief and an inevitable enemy. Further, these moderates are increasingly susceptible to the influence of the powerful minority of Islamic extremists.

There are also millions of adherents of Islam who increasingly view America, and the West generally, with suspicion and distrust, sometimes even hatred. The reasons for this are complex and many, but in general they have to do with

- resentment toward the success of the West and the desire for the "glory" of the Islamic past—a return to a "unified" Islamic empire

- Islam's traditional placement of the world into only two basic divisions—"the land of Islam" *(dar al-Islam)*, and "the land of the unbeliever," or heretic *(dar al-harb)*, the latter eventually destined for absorption or conquest by the former

- a bias in the Quran against the Jews (Suras 3:187-89; 4:160-61; 5:82; 62:5-8; but see 5:13; 20:159), compounded by the Israeli-Palestinian conflict, in which Muslims see the State of Israel as an invader and occupier of land that by divine right belongs to Arabs (again, as promised in the Quran)

- the frustration and plight of most Muslims, who in general live in Third World countries—but who do not see that Islam itself is largely responsible for their condition. (Probably 50 percent of all Muslims globally live in abject poverty.[12])

- Muslims' perceived, in some cases valid, grievances against some moderate or secular Arab governments

- the conversion of significant numbers of Muslims to Christianity in various places around the world, which is seen by many Muslims as a substantial threat to the expansion of Islam

- America's increasing secularism, relativism, and rejection of moral values, which many Muslims (like many Christians) aren't at all happy with

- last but not least, the increasing influence of radical Islam, which hopes to take advantage of all the above and which furthermore hopes to radicalize Islam by overthrowing moderate or secular Muslim governments, gaining increasing power, and finally confronting or destroying the "corrupt," "satanic" West and its dominant power, America.

A Minority?

Some have argued that those elements within Islam that hate America and the West constitute a very small minority of "crazy zealots" (such as Osama bin Laden and his followers) having no lasting relevance or consequence to the world. These "minimizers," however, "severely underestimate the penetration of extremist doctrine within much of mainstream Islam, especially in the Arab world."[13]

Regardless of this, since we are talking about 1.3 billion adherents to Islam, even a "very small minority" can involve tens of millions of people who have the potential to cause a great deal of trouble in the world, not only for America, but for moderate Muslim governments as well. Islam authority Dr.

Daniel Pipes argues that radicals comprise "perhaps 10 to 15 percent of the [Muslim] population. Many of them are peaceable in appearance, but they all must be considered potential killers."[14] That could be as many as 200 million people.

Many have emphasized that we are not in a war of civilizations—that most Muslims just aren't interested in *jihad* or *dar al-Islam* versus *dar al-harb*. While this might be true enough, we still may be entering the beginning of such a clash of civilizations that will involve at least significant portions of the Muslim world. And it would not take the involvement of a majority of believers to still cause more trouble than anyone needs.

Part of the problem is that it can be difficult to gauge exactly where a large majority of Muslims worldwide stand on critical issues. For example, according to the television news program *60 Minutes*, even in the "moderate" Arab world there is widespread anger, even hatred toward the U.S. (and public sentiment is strong, though not universal, that America "deserved" what happened in the September 11 attack).

What Does "Moderate" Mean?

Some now wonder what "moderate" really means anymore when "moderate" Arab newspapers have carried articles like the one below from the Kuwaiti *Al-Watan* (from September 1, 2001). Although the article was written to justify the killing of Israeli women and children, the reasons given are applicable to the killing of women and children in any country with which Islam is at war.

> ...The second case when the killing of civilians and women is permitted is when Muslims must launch a comprehensive attack against their enemies or shoot them from afar....Among these attacks are the [suicide] martyrdom attacks that aim to kill...in order to strike terror in their hearts....In these attacks some women and children are unintentionally killed, of course, but this

is with full right. [Otherwise] it would [lead] to the paralyzing of Jihad for the sake of Allah....It is impossible to avoid killing civilians in a war....[15]

According to noted columnist Cal Thomas,

Most Arab newspapers are either controlled by, or supportive of, their respective dictatorial governments. One wonders how serious these governments are about fighting terroism when inflammatory editorials appear. Columnist Mahmoud Abd Al-Mun'im Murad, of the Egyptian-government sponsored daily *Al-Akhbar,* wrote recently, "The Statue of Liberty in New York Harbor must be destroyed..." This venom comes from a supposedly "moderate" Arab country. It is much worse in other media throughout the Arab world.[16]

If such thinking is increasingly representative of "moderate" Muslims, then perhaps Islam itself is what the world must take note of, not just Muslim radicals and terrorists.

Why Is the West a Target?

Why is the U.S.—indeed, the entire West—a target for Muslim radicals? Muslim fundamentalism–radicalism is often said to be the result of economic, political, or social grievances. While true in part, this is an oversimplification that fails to understand the forces operating within Islam. Poverty can't explain Muslim terrorism because the same or worse conditions for Christians in Brazil or Mexico have not resulted in their engaging in international acts of terror.

Nor is the Arab–Jewish conflict in Israel the root of the problem. Anti-American hatred exists—even the killing of Christians occurs—in countries and cultures far removed from the Middle East conflict, such as the Sudan, Afghanistan, and Nigeria. Furthermore, *jihad* is aimed primarily at America and the West, not Israel.

We cannot truly understand how radical Muslims view the U.S. and the West until we understand how they view the *world*. Remember that in their worldview there are only two divisions: the land of Islam, and the land of unbelievers. What the radicals want is a new world; manipulating local conflicts is just a means to an end.

> Within this conception *[dar al-Islam* versus *dar al-harb]*, Islam's mission is to bring the true faith to the whole of mankind. In pursuit of this goal, Islamic radicals and fundamentalists (Islamists) resort to a variety of tactics, from education, propaganda, economic and spiritual guidance, to political subversion, terror and war. An analysis of the foci of conflict shows that the Islamists' primary concern is to reshape the political reality within the Muslim world.[17]

And the radicals are working constantly to reshape Muslim opinion toward their goals. Given our misunderstandings of Islam, the West has some important reassessment to undertake, and quickly. Many people today hesitate to speak of "Muslim terrorism" or "Islamic terrorism." But the enormity of what has occurred—and the future health of the world—require it.

Before we proceed with our discussion of Islam's relationship to today's world, in order to better comprehend the nature of the worldview clash we will take a look at traditional Islam's religious beliefs, its Bible, and the credibility of its evidential claims.

The Theology of Islam: Is It Compatible with Christian Belief?

What Does Islam Teach About God (Allah)?

Islam teaches that the true God is the Muslim deity, Allah. All other views of God are false because the Quran teaches, "The true religion with God is Islam."[18] Thus the Quran emphasizes of Allah, "There is no God but he, the Living, the everlasting."[19]

But who is Allah? Is he similar to the God of the Christian faith? First, the Quran stresses that Allah is one person only:

> They are unbelievers who say, "God is the Third of Three." No god is there but one God. If they refrain not from what they say, there shall afflict those of them that disbelieve a painful chastisement."[20]

Here, the Quran emphasizes that Christians are considered unbelievers because they accept the historic Christian doctrine of the Trinity.[21] However, the Bible unmistakably teaches that God has revealed Himself as a triune Being, as One God eternally existing in three Persons—Father, Son, and Holy Spirit

(Mt. 28:19; Jn. 1:1,14; Acts 5:3-4).[22] Although many Muslims think otherwise, Christians do not believe in three gods. Christians are not polytheists, but monotheists who believe in one God.

Allah also has a different character than the biblical God. It is significant, that of the "99 beautiful names for Allah," which Muslims memorize and use for worship, not one of these names is "love" or "loving." The Quran stresses that Allah only loves those who do good, and that he does not love those who are bad. Allah does *not* love the sinner.[23] Thus, the love of Allah and the love of the God of the Bible are distinct from each other. The biblical God does love the sinner—in fact, He loves all sinners. God does not love the sin, but He does love the sinner:

> Christ died for the *ungodly*....God *demonstrates* his own *love* for us in this: While we were *still sinners,* Christ died for us....If, when we were God's *enemies,* we were reconciled to him through the death of his Son, how much more, having been reconciled, shall we be saved through his life! (Rom. 5:6,8,10).

Allah is primarily a God of transcendence and power, not a God of love. But the Bible declares, "God *is* love" (1 Jn. 4:8).

Can Allah Be Known?

Allah is ultimately unknowable and incomprehensible. In *Who Is Allah in Islam?* Abd-al-Masih writes, "Allah is the unique, unexplorable, and inexplicable one—the remote, vast, and unknown God. Everything we think about him is incomplete, if not wrong. Allah cannot be comprehended."[24] This stands in contrast to the biblical teaching that men and women can know God personally on an intimate, relational level. Consider these Scriptures: "This is eternal life, that they may know You, the only true God, and Jesus Christ whom You have sent" (Jn. 17:3). Jesus said, "my sheep know me" (Jn. 10:14). The apostle Paul prayed for Christian believers concerning God, "that you may *know* him better" (Eph. 1:17). The apostle John emphasized, "Dear friends, let us love one another, for love comes from God. Everyone who loves has been born of God and *knows* God. Whoever does not love does not know God, because God is love" (1 Jn. 4:7-8).

In "What Is Allah Like?" George Houssney writes,

> We humans can never know Allah, because he is so far from us and so different from us. The only knowledge Muslims may admit to is knowledge about Allah, not a personal, experiential knowledge of him. People cannot know Allah and should not even try to know him. Allah is not involved in the affairs of humans....The Christian claim that humans can have a relationship with God is considered by Muslims to be a metaphysical impossibility. To Muslims, Allah has not revealed himself, but rather he has revealed his *mashi'at* (desires and wishes, i.e., his will). His will, according to Islamic teaching, is limited to Islamic law. A person performs the will of Allah when he follows the dictates of the Islamic legal system.[25]

WHAT DOES ISLAM TEACH ABOUT JESUS CHRIST?

Muslims maintain that they believe in the true Jesus Christ. They praise Jesus as a prophet of God, as sinless, as "the Messiah," as "illustrious in this world and the next," as "the Word of Allah," and as "the Spirit of God."[26] Islam believes that Jesus was merely one of God's many prophets or messengers, not God's only Son. Muslims cite the Quran in confirmation of their belief in Jesus, for example, "And we gave Jesus, Son of Mary, the clear signs, and confirmed Him with the Holy Spirit."[27]

Islam accepts what is taught about Jesus in the Quran, rather than what is taught about Jesus in the Bible, because it believes the Quran is the pure Word of God and that the Bible is corrupted and is therefore wrong in its teachings about Jesus.

The Quran teaches:

> They say, "God has taken to Him a son."…Say: "Those who forge against God falsehood shall not prosper."[28]

> Warn those who say, "God has taken to Himself a son";…a monstrous word it is, issuing out of their mouths; they say nothing but a lie.[29]

> But who does greater evil than he who forges against God a lie?[30]

> They are unbelievers who say, "God is the Messiah, Mary's Son."[31]

The Christian view of Jesus Christ as God's Son is considered blasphemous to the Muslim.[32] Sura 5:72,75 reads, "They do blaspheme who say: 'God is Christ the son of Mary.'… Christ the son of Mary was no more than an apostle."[33]

This is so because the Quran emphasizes that Jesus was only a man. Sura 43:59 asserts: "Jesus was no more than a mortal whom [Allah] favored and made an example to the Israelites."

Obviously, then, Muslims deny that Jesus Christ was God incarnate (see Jn. 5:18; 19:7). A Muslim who believes that Jesus Christ is God has committed an unforgivable sin called *shirk*—the association of another god with Allah, a sin that will send the Muslim to hell forever, as the Quran emphasizes: "His abode is the Fire" (Sura 5:72).[34] The Quran teaches, "Muhammad…is the last prophet and messenger of Allah. His mission was for the whole world and for all times" (4:35). In essence, Muslims must look only to Muhammad's revelation for spiritual guidance, not to Jesus.

What Does the Bible Say About Jesus?

The Bible, of course, teaches that Jesus is God's one and only Son. Jesus Himself taught this, for example, "God so loved the world that he gave his one and only Son, that whoever believes in him shall not perish but have eternal life....Whoever believes in him is not condemned, but whoever does not believe stands condemned already because he has not believed in the name of God's one and only Son" (Jn. 3:16,18; cf. Mt. 11:27; 26:64).

God the Father declared this of Jesus at His baptism. "A voice from heaven said, 'This is my Son, whom I love; with him I am well pleased'" (Mt. 3:17; cf. 17:5). The apostles Paul and John also declared that Jesus is God's Son (Rom. 1:3; 1 Jn. 5:9-12). In fact, virtually every book in the New Testament either declares or assumes that Jesus is God's unique Son.

Biblically, Jesus Christ is far more than one of God's messengers or prophets. Jesus Himself claimed He was God on many different occasions. He is the second Person of the Trinity, God incarnate—Deity Himself (Jn. 1:1,14; 5:18). Jesus claimed to be both the "Lord" and "God": "You call me 'Teacher' and 'Lord,' and rightly so, for that is what I am" (Jn. 13:13). "Anyone who has seen me has seen the Father [God]" (Jn. 14:9). "I and the Father [God] are one" (Jn. 10:30).

The Quran rejects this and has Jesus denying His own deity. When Allah asks Jesus if He is God, Jesus replies, "It is not mine to say what I have no right to."[35] In fact, even as a baby, Jesus allegedly claimed He was only a servant of Allah. According to Sura 19:20,34, Jesus praised his birth and then said, "I am the servant of Allah."

WHAT DOES ISLAM TEACH
ABOUT SALVATION?

Because the Quran teaches that "the true religion with God is Islam,"[36] salvation is achieved only through submission to the teachings of Allah. Salvation in Islam requires that one must be a member of the Islamic faith. "Whoso desires another religion than Islam, it shall not be accepted of him; in the next world he shall be among the losers."[37] Thus, "those who disbelieve, and die disbelieving—upon them shall rest the curse of God and the angels, and of men altogether, there indwelling forever; the chastisement shall not be lightened for them; no respite shall be given them."[38]

Below are three basic points that illustrate what the religion of Islam teaches about salvation.

Forgiveness

Islam teaches that forgiveness is conditioned upon good works and Allah's choice of mercy.

Muslims believe that by striving to please God and by doing good works, they will hopefully gain entrance to heaven through personal merit. The Quran clearly teaches that salvation is achieved on the basis of meritorious good works and personal righteousness. Consider the following:

> ...every soul shall be paid in full what it has earned....[39]

> ...God loves those who cleanse themselves.[40]

> Gardens of Eden, underneath which rivers flow, there indwelling forever; that is the recompense of the self-purified.[41]

Islam teaches that on the Day of Judgment one's good and evil deeds will be weighed on a scale. Good works are heavy and evil deeds are light. The Quran asserts:

> [In the Day of Judgment] they whose balances shall be heavy with good works, shall be happy; but they whose balances shall be light, are those who shall lose their souls, and shall remain in hell forever. [42]

The Muslim assumes that his chances for heaven are good if he 1) accepts only the Muslim God Allah and his prophet Muhammad, 2) does good works and all that is required of him by Allah (for example, the Pillars of Religion), and 3) if he also is predestined to heaven by Allah's favor. No Muslim can have an assurance of salvation, because he has no ultimate guarantee of either the weight of his good works or the final favor of Allah.

The Bible emphasizes that salvation does not come by good works or anything else we can do to please God on our own efforts: "We maintain that a man is justified by faith apart from observing the law" (Rom. 3:28). "It is by grace you have been saved, through faith—and this *not from yourselves,* it is the gift of God—*not by works,* so that no one can boast" (Eph. 2:8-9).

The Bible's View of Forgiveness

The Muslim concept of forgiveness stands in contrast to that of biblical Christianity, where forgiveness involves a free gift of God's grace and mercy as a past action, based on the death of Christ on the cross for sin. This means that, once a person receives Christ as his or her Savior, all sins are forgiven (Col. 2:14) and that person is guaranteed a place in heaven:

> I tell you the truth, whoever hears my word and believes him who sent me has eternal life and will not be condemned (Jn. 5:24).

> Praise be to the God and Father of our Lord Jesus Christ! In his great mercy he has given us new birth into a living hope through the resurrection of Jesus Christ from the dead, and into an inheritance that can never perish, spoil or fade—kept in heaven for you, who through faith are shielded by God's power until the coming of the salvation that is ready to be revealed in the last time (1 Pet. 1:3-5).

The Bible teaches of Jesus, "He Himself bore our sins in His body on the cross, so that we might die to sin and live to righteousness" (1 Pet. 2:24), and "He is the atoning sacrifice for our sins" (1 Jn. 2:2). Indeed, "God presented him [Jesus] as a sacrifice of atonement" and "[God] did it to demonstrate his justice at the present time, so as to be just and the one who justifies those who have faith in Jesus" (Rom. 3:26). Thus, "He forgave us *all* our sins" (Col. 2:13).

In Islam, there is no atonement for sin—no propitiatory basis for forgiveness of sins. Allah simply forgives whom he chooses to forgive. The following statements in the Quran, as well as many others, indicate the conditional nature of Islamic forgiveness:

> God will not forgive those who serve other gods besides him; but he will forgive whom he will for other sins. He that serves other gods besides God is guilty of a heinous sin.[43]

> Some shall be damned and others shall be blessed.... The damned shall be cast into the Fire unless your Lord ordain otherwise: your Lord shall accomplish what He will. As for the blessed, they shall abide in Paradise as long as the heavens and the earth endure, unless your Lord ordain otherwise.[44]

To the contrary, the Bible teaches that we can have the assurance of having received eternal life. The apostle John emphasized, "I write these things to you who believe in the name of the Son of God so that you may *know* that you *have* eternal life" (1 Jn. 5:13).

Jesus' Crucifixion and Resurrection

Islam teaches that Jesus Christ was neither crucified nor resurrected; therefore, it is impossible that salvation can be had through faith in Christ.

Islam does not accept the atoning sacrifice of Jesus Christ on the cross. If Jesus did not die on the cross, He obviously did not die on the cross for sin. Islam believes that mankind is basically good; thus, if humans are not unredeemed sinners, they do not need redemption from sin and a savior from sin—only good works, abstention from wickedness, and Allah's favor. Also, it is unthinkable that God would permit one of His prophets to be crucified. The Quran teaches,

> They denied the truth and uttered a monstrous falsehood….They declared: "We have put to death the Messiah, Jesus the son of Mary, the apostle of Allah." They did not kill him, nor did they crucify him, but they thought they did.[45]

Muslims therefore believe that God substituted someone else on the cross in Jesus' place.

But Jesus Himself prophesied—repeatedly—that He had to go to the cross, that it was to atone for sin, and that He would be resurrected from the dead—and that this was God's direct will for Him. Jesus taught of Himself that "the Son of Man did not come to be served, but to serve, and to give his life as a ransom for many" (Mt. 20:28).

Jesus took the twelve disciples aside and told them,

> We are going up to Jerusalem, and everything that is written by the prophets about the Son of Man will be fulfilled. He will be handed over to the Gentiles. They will mock him, insult him, spit on him, flog him and kill him. On the third day he will rise again (Lk. 18:31-33).

And He spoke again of Himself, "Now my heart is troubled, and what shall I say? 'Father, save me from this hour'? No, it was for this very reason I came to this hour" (Jn. 12:27).

Denial of the Resurrection

Innumerable eyewitnesses, both Jesus' friends and enemies, saw Him die on the cross (Jn. 19:23-27, 31-35). Further, many of His disciples and friends were also eyewitnesses to His resurrection from the dead, confirming His claim to be the Son of God (Rom. 1:3).

Because Muslims do not believe that Christ died on the cross, they logically deny His resurrection. Ahmad Dedat is one of the leading public defenders of Islam. He claims that

> throughout the length and breadth of the 27 books of the New Testament, there is not a single statement made by Jesus Christ that "I was dead, and I have come back from the dead." The Christian has [wrongly] been belaboring the word resurrection. Again and again, by repetition, it is conveyed that it [the resurrection] is proving a fact....[But] Jesus Christ never uttered the word that "I have come back from the dead," in the 27 books of the New Testament, not once.[46]

But Mr. Dedat is mistaken. On a dozen different occasions Jesus predicted both His death *and* His resurrection. For example, He told His disciples, "The Son of Man must suffer many things and be rejected by the elders, chief priests and teachers of the law, and he must be killed *and on the third day be raised to life*" (Lk. 9:22). After His resurrection He said to His disciples,

> This was what I told you while I was still with you: Everything must be fulfilled that is written about me in the Law of Moses, the Prophets and the Psalms....This is what is written: The Christ will suffer and rise from the dead on the third day, and repentance and forgiveness of sins will be preached in his name to all nations (Lk. 24:44,46,47).

Fatalism

Muslim salvation is fatalistic, especially in regard to the indeterminacy of Allah's predestination.

The Quran teaches, "All things have we created after a fixed decree...." Further, "God leads astray whomsoever He will; and He guides whomsoever He will...."[47] Abdiyah Akbar Abdul-Haqq observes:

There are several [Muslim] traditions also about the predestination of all things, including all good and bad actions and guided and misguided people.... Even if a person desires to choose God's guidance, he cannot do so without the prior choice of God in favor of his free choice. This is sheer determinism.[48]

Dr. Wilson comments,

The fifth article of [Muslim] faith is predestination,...the fact that everything that happens, either good or bad, is foreordained by the unchangeable decrees of Allah. It will be seen at once that this makes Allah the author of evil, a doctrine that most Muslim theologians hold.[49]

The Quran teaches, for example, "And if a good thing visits them, they say, 'This is from God'; but if an evil thing visits them, they say, 'This is from thee.' Say: 'Everything is from God.'"[50] And,

The man whom Allah guides is rightly guided, but he who is led astray by Allah shall surely be lost. As for those that deny Our revelations, We have pre-destined for hell many jinn [evil spirits] and many men....We will lead them step by step to ruin.... None can guide the people whom Allah leads astray. He leaves them blundering about in their wickedness....Say: "I have not the power to acquire benefits or to avert evil from myself, except by the will of Allah."[51]

Jihad—a Guarantee?

At first glance there does appear to be one way a Muslim can guarantee his salvation. This is found in connection with the Muslim concept of *jihad*, or holy war. (See questions 21–23 and 31 for a longer discussion of the issues of *jihad*.) Achieving security of salvation requires death in battle while defending Islam: "If you are slain or die in God's way...it is unto God you shall be mustered...."[52]

> When you meet the unbelievers in the battlefields strike off their heads and, when you have laid them low, bind your captives firmly....Thus shall you do....As for those who are slain in the cause of Allah...he will admit them to the Paradise he has made known to them.[53]

> Allah has given those that fight with their goods and their persons a higher rank than those who stay at home....The unbelievers are your sworn enemies....Seek out your enemies relentlessly.... You shall not plead for traitors....Allah does not love the treacherous or the sinful.[54]

It appears at first that the Muslim is promised heaven for death in battle. But we discover that this security of salvation appears to be conditioned on accompanying bravery. (This was seen in the admonitions given to the September 11 terrorists—see question 26.) Thus:

> O believers, when you encounter the unbelievers marching to battle, turn not your backs to them. Whoso turns his back that day to them, unless withdrawing to fight again or removing to join another host, he is laden with the burden of God's anger, and his refuge is Gehenna—an evil home-coming![55]

Even in the guarantee of heaven through death in a holy war, the Muslim promise of salvation is provisional. And none can deny that unnumbered Muslims, trusting in Islam to save them and take them to Paradise, have instead been sent to their deaths in the *jihads* of history and today. They have been sent to eternity without Christ.

CAN MUSLIMS AND CHRISTIANS ENGAGE IN REWARDING DIALOG?

Both Muslims and Christians have directed sustained apologetic efforts toward one another (for example, see Answering-Islam.org). Clearly, whatever good may otherwise exist within these religions, two opposing belief systems cannot both be correct. Both might be false, or one might be true, but both can't ultimately be true at the same time. This can become a path to learning for those who believe that truth has nothing to fear from inquiry.

Unfortunately, Muslims have a number of misunderstandings about Christianity that can cause great difficulty. Muslims may also be very sensitive to even valid criticisms of Islam, the Quran, or the prophet Muhammad, so dialog can be difficult. (Help on effectively relating to Muslims—"dos" and "don'ts," and more—can be found in the note preceding the endnotes and in the resource list. We emphasize that any Christian desiring to work with Muslims will find it helpful to continue studies in this direction.)

This underscores the importance of Christians and Muslims understanding one another in conversation, and the importance of honest interpretation of historical, textual, and other data. As Christians, we have read detailed Muslim critiques of our faith. We hope that Muslims will be willing to do the same. Indeed, neither Christians nor Muslims know who might become their friends in this life. But Christians know for a fact that God's love is wide and broad, and can reach into corners where many would fear to tread. Indeed, even for radical Muslim terrorists who are filled with hatred, there is still hope. As the Quran teaches in Sura 60:7, "It may be that Allah will bring about friendship between you and those of them whom you hold as enemies. And Allah is Powerful; and Allah is Forgiving, Merciful."[56]

In short, even critical religious dialogue will be possible among those who seek it and are willing to subject their own religious traditions to fair-minded analysis.

The Bible of Islam: Is the Quran the Word of God?

11

What Does Islam Claim About the Quran?

Muslims believe the Quran is perfect and without error. Muslims Musa Qutub, Ph.D., and M. Vazir Ali assert that the Quran is the only book ever to "withstand the microscopic and telescopic scrutiny of one and all, without the book stumbling anywhere."[57]

Islam further claims that the teachings of the Quran are in harmony with the autographs of the Bible, because this is what the Quran teaches. (Again, it believes Christians have corrupted the Bible, so that the Bibles Christians now use are unreliable.)

> ...And We have sent down to thee the Book [the Quran] with the truth, confirming the Book [the Bible] that was before it, and assuring it.[58]

> This Quran could not have been forged apart from God; but it is a *confirmation* of what is before it....[59]

12

DO THE QURAN AND THE BIBLE AGREE, AND WHY DOES THIS MATTER?

Anyone who carefully examines both the Bible and the Quran would admit that, as they stand, they contradict one another on every major religious doctrine: the nature of God, Jesus, salvation, mankind, Scripture, and others. If the New Testament was *not* corrupted (question 17), then Muslims need to explain how Allah could be the inspiration behind *both* 1) the Bible *and* 2) the Quran, which contradicts it.

13

IS THE QURAN HISTORICALLY ACCURATE?

Muslims and Christians agree that it is impossible for God to inspire error in His Word. The Quran, however, contains a large number of statements that contradict the Bible. (Again, how could Allah be the inspiration behind *both* books?) Dr. Robert Morey lists more than 100 contradictions; for example, citing A. Yusuf Ali's translation (one accepted by Muslims), the Quran teaches that the ark of Noah came to rest on the top of Mt. Judi (Sura 11:44), not Mt. Ararat as the Bible teaches; that Abraham's father was Azar (Sura 6:74), not Terah as the Bible teaches; that he attempted to sacrifice Ishmael (Sura 37:100-112), not Isaac as the Bible teaches; that Pharaoh's *wife* adopted Moses (Sura 28:8-9), not his daughter as the Bible teaches; that Noah's flood occurred in Moses' day (Sura 7:136, cf., 7:59ff.); that Mary, the mother of Jesus, gave birth to Jesus under a palm tree (Sura 19:22), not in a stable as the Bible teaches; that Mary's father was named Imram (Sura 66:12); and many more.[60]

In the preface to his translation of the Quran, Rodwell notes the presence of "contradictory and…inaccurate statements."[61] For example, Muhammad is nowhere found in the Bible, but the Quran claims that Muhammad himself is "described in the Torah and the Gospel."[62] The disciples of Christ were obviously Christians, but the Quran teaches that the disciples of Christ were Muslims. Six hundred years before Muhammad was born, Christ's disciples allegedly declare, "We believe; and bear thou witness that we are Muslims."[63]

The Quran also teaches that Abraham was not a Jew, but a Muslim. "No; Abraham in truth was not a Jew, neither a Christian; but he was a Muslim…."[64]

There are also some things that are difficult to interpret in the Quran. After Allah tempts the people to sin in judgment for their evil, "when they had scornfully persisted in what they had been forbidden, We changed them into detested apes."[65] According to history, the army of the king of Ethiopia, Abraha, halted its attack on Mecca due to a smallpox outbreak. Sura 105 teaches he was defeated by birds that dropped stones of baked clay on the soldiers.

As noted, the Quran has many biblical distortions.[66] Almost every biblical episode discussed in the Quran has additional or contrary information, or both, supplied. For example, in Sura 2:56,57,61 the Jews returned to Egypt *after* the Exodus, which, biblically and historically, was never the case. In Sura 3:41 it is stated that Zechariah would be speechless for three days. Biblically, it was until John's birth—nine months (Lk. 1:18-20). In Sura 12:11-20 the Quranic story of Joseph is markedly different from the biblical story of Genesis 37; the accounts are so contrary as to demand that one be in error. In Sura 2:241, Muhammad confuses the persons of Saul and Gideon. There are also variations in Sura 12:21-32,36-55 when compared with Genesis 37–45.[67]

Whether it is the descriptions of the creation of man, the Fall, Moses and the burning bush, Noah and the ark, Joseph going into Egypt, or the lives of Zechariah, John the Baptist, Mary and Jesus, or other biblical characters, the Quran often contradicts biblical teaching.[68] Nonetheless, the Quran also explicitly claims to "confirm the Book of Moses and the Gospel."[69]

Is the Quran Self-Contradictory?

The Quran emphasizes that it contains no contradictions. In Sura 4:84 Allah challenges men, "Will they not ponder on the Quran? If it had not come from Allah, they could have surely found in it many contradictions."[70] If Allah does not contradict himself, then everything that has purportedly "come down from him" (the Bible, the Quran) must be in agreement. The Muslim must believe in the doctrinal unity of the books of Allah—the Bible as originally given and the Quran. But we have just seen they conflict. Muslims counter this by asserting that the Bible's text is corrupted, but without supplying any credible evidence to back their claims.

Even so, the Quran contains contradictions within its own pages. For example, in Sura 11 it teaches that one of Noah's sons didn't go into the ark, and thus "Noah's son was drowned" in the Flood.[71] The Quran then contradicts this statement in Sura 21, where it declares that "we saved him [Noah] and *all* his kinsfolk from the great calamity...."[72] (According to the Bible, all of Noah's sons were delivered [Gen. 6–8].)

ISLAM:
A GENERAL CRITIQUE

15

ARE MUSLIM APOLOGETICS CONVINCING?

The word "apologetics" is derived from the Greek *apologia,* which means "to present a defense for."

In "How Muslims Do Apologetics," trial attorney, philosopher, and theologian Dr. John Warwick Montgomery discusses a characteristic problem of Muslim apologetics—that of defending Islam by "discrediting" Christianity. But "such refutations are not 'apologies' or defenses at all, but are *ad hominem* arguments of an offensive nature."[73]

Even if Muslim apologists could disprove Christianity, this would not prove the truth of Islam. Islam would still require— on its own merits—independent verification as a revelation of God. And because the evidence is lacking, it is precisely at this point that Muslim apologists fail—one can never prove true what has already been determined untrue. However, biblical inspiration and accuracy are independently verified by prophecy, archeology, manuscript evidence, and other means. (We documented this in some detail in *Ready with an Answer* [Harvest House, 1997]).

Islam offers no trustworthy evidence for its claim that the Quran is inspired, other than Muhammad's personal claim. What if Muhammad was wrong?

Muslims argue that the Christian faith is a false religion. First, using the discredited arguments of liberal theologians, of proponents of higher critical methods (for example, "form criticism"), and of atheistic or rationalistic skeptics of Christianity, they reject biblical authority and the deity of Christ.[74] Second, they present arguments in defense of Islam that seem to convince Muslims, but that are discredited upon examination or are primarily subjective and therefore prove very little.[75]

Third, many Christian scholars and students of the Bible have evaluated the arguments of leading Muslim apologists and refuted them. (See Resource List, especially Web sites.)

WHAT BASIC PROBLEM DOES THE QURAN PRESENT FOR MUSLIMS?

As we have indicated, the Quran teaches that Muslims are to accept both the Bible and the Quran.

> Say: "We believe in God, and that which has been sent down on us, *and* sent down on Abraham and Ishmael, Isaac and Jacob, and the [Jewish] Tribes, and in that which was given to Moses and Jesus, and the Prophets, of their Lord; *we make no division between any of them....*"[76]

The Quran claims that Allah is the God who inspired the Old and New Testaments: "...We gave to Moses the Book and the Salvation, that haply you should be guided."[77] Muslims are commanded, "Observe the Torah and the Gospel...what is revealed to them from Allah."[78]

Elsewhere Muslims are told,

> O believers, believe in God and His Messenger
> [Muhammad] and the Book He has sent down on
> His Messenger [the Quran] and the Book which
> He sent down before [the Bible]. Whoso disbelieves
> in God and His angels and His Books, and His
> Messengers, and the Last Day, has surely gone
> astray into far error....God will gather the hyp-
> ocrites and the unbelievers all in Gehenna.[79]

In the above verses we see that those who reject God's "Books" (plural) and "Messengers" (plural) are declared to be unbelievers![80] Muslims are forbidden by Allah to accept only part of His revelations. But here is the dilemma. If Muslims accept what the Quran teaches, they must then accept what the Bible teaches—which rejects what the Quran teaches.

But if a Muslim truly accepts the Bible and rejects what the Quran teaches, he or she can no longer remain a Muslim and should become a Christian.[81] One wonders how a Muslim can logically trust what the Quran teaches, when it thereby undermines its own authority. This difficulty cannot be circumvented by claiming that the Bible's teachings have been corrupted and are therefore untrustworthy, without offering evidence of the corruption.

IS THE MUSLIM CLAIM THAT THE BIBLE IS CORRUPTED BASED ON FACT?

The Quran claims that the Bible has been corrupted by Christians: "People of the Book [Jews and Christians], now there has come to you Our Messenger [Muhammad], making clear to you many things you have been concealing of the Book, and defacing many things."[82]

In his *Christian Faith and Other Faiths*, Oxford theologian Stephen Neill observes,

> It is well known that at many points the Quran
> does not agree with the Jewish and Christian Scrip-
> tures. Therefore, from the Muslim point of view, it
> follows of necessity that these Scriptures must have
> been corrupted. Historical evidence makes no
> impression on the crushing force of the syllogism.
> So it is, and it can be no other way. The Muslim
> controversialist feels no need to study evidence in
> detail. The only valid picture of Jesus Christ is that
> which is to be found in the pages of the Quran.[83]

In other words, because the Quran is predefined as God's
perfect revelation and the Bible contradicts it, the Bible must
be corrupted. Historical evidence has no relevance to the issue
because it is impossible that the Quran could be wrong.[84]

This is placing the cart before the horse. One must first
determine if the Bible was corrupted. If not, then the error
must lie with the Quran. And historical facts prove that the
Bible has not been corrupted.[85] If Muslims are not willing to
truthfully examine and accept this evidence, it can hardly be
considered the fault of Christians.

For example, after a thorough evaluation of the textual evidence, and citing numerous scholars in confirmation, Drs.
Norman Geisler and William Nix conclude that a modern critical edition of the Bible says "exactly what the autographs con-
tained—line for line, word for word, and even letter for letter."[86]

In regard to the New Testament, anyone who wishes can
prove to his or her own satisfaction that, on the basis of
accepted bibliographic, internal, external, and other criteria,
its text can be established to be original, without corruption.
Textually, we know we have over 99 percent of the autographs
(the remaining 1 percent, about half a page, exists in variant
readings). Furthermore, the methods used by biblical critics
that Muslims rely on (rationalist, "higher critical" methods),
which claim "assured results" that allegedly prove the New
Testament unreliable, have been weighed in the balance of

secular scholarship and found wanting. Fair-minded biblical critics would have to agree that higher criticism's 200-year failure to prove its case by default strengthens the Christian view as to biblical reliability.

Evidence for Reliability

Today, of the New Testament, there are 5,300 Greek manuscripts and portions; 10,000 Latin Vulgate; plus 9,300 copies of other versions. In fact, the papyri manuscripts and early uncial manuscripts of the New Testament date much closer to the original than is the case with any other ancient literature. This proves, by physical, textual means, that the New Testament text has not been corrupted. In addition, consider these points—

- The lack of proven fraud or error on the part of any New Testament author—despite 2,000 years of challenges—establishes that the writers were trustworthy in what they wrote.
- The writings of reliable Christian sources outside the New Testament help confirm its integrity.
- Detailed, critical, archeological investigation, such as that by Sir William Ramsay, proves the authors wrote with care and accuracy.
- None of the powerful first-century enemies of Jesus and the apostolic church were ever able to prove fraud. To the contrary, the presence of numerous, credible, living eyewitnesses to the events recorded, especially to Jesus' death and resurrection, offers substantial corroborating evidence for the truth of what was recorded, since the witnesses were willing to die for their claims.
- There are powerful appraisals by conservative, and even some liberal, authorities that bear on the issue of the genuineness of the traditional authorship and the early date of the New Testament books, further confirming their integrity.
- Finally, there is weighty testimony from legal argument as to New Testament reliability.

We have discussed each of these points and provided documentation for them in our *Ready with an Answer* and *The*

Facts on the Reliability of the Bible (both Harvest House, 1997). In essence, the Muslim claim that the New Testament has been corrupted textually is not only untrue, but it can never be substantiated because of the nature of the textual and other evidence at hand.

We can only hope that open-minded Muslims will impartially investigate the evidence for the New Testament's authenticity. In the past, Muslims have done this many times and have been surprised at what they have found.

IS THE QURAN UNCORRUPTED?

Historical facts demonstrate that the Quran's text is corrupt in a number of ways. First, the Quran is not written in perfect Arabic (cf. Sura 12:2; 13:37; 41:41,44), but has scores of grammatical errors and non-Arabic words.[87] Sources such as *The Origins of the Quran: Classic Essays on Islam's Holy Book,* (editor Ibn Warraq), though sometimes displaying a rationalistic bias, nevertheless prove beyond doubt that the Quran is not a pure text.

> Muslim scholars of the early years [knew]…there were many thousand variants which made it impossible to talk of the Koran.…Jeffrey, chapter 6, has listed fifteen primary codices.…[Worse], the consonantal text was unpointed, [leading to]…a great many [additional] variant readings.… [Charles Adams says] these variants affected even the [standardized] 'Uthmanic codex, making it difficult to know what its true form may have been.…Hadiths [sayings of Muhammad] were… fabricated even for the most trivial ritualistic details.[88]

Dr. Robert Morey, who who has debated leading Muslim apologists on several occasions, points out that

> there are many differing readings of the text of the Quran as Arthur Jeffrey has demonstrated in his book *Material for the History of the Text of the Quran*. At one point, Jeffrey gives 90 pages of variant readings. For example, in Sura 2 there are over 140 conflicting and variant readings....
>
> All Western and Muslim scholars admit the presence of variant readings.... According to Professor Guillaume in his book *Islam* (pp. 191ff.), some of the original verses of the Quran were lost. For example, one Sura originally had 200 verses in the days of Ayesha. But by the time Uthman standardized the text of the Quran, it had only 73 verses! A total of 127 verses had been lost, and they have never been recovered. The Shiite Muslims claim that Uthman left out 25 percent of the original verses in the Quran for political reasons....
>
> John Burton's book, *The Collection of the Quran*, which was published by Cambridge University, documents how such verses were lost. Burton states concerning the Muslim claim that the Quran is perfect: "The Muslim accounts of the history of the Quran texts are a mass of confusion, contradictions and inconsistencies...."
>
> ...Not only have parts of the Quran been lost, but entire verses and chapters have been added to it. For example, Ubai had several Suras in his manuscript of the Quran which Uthman omitted from his standardized text. Thus there were Qurans in circulation before Uthman's text which had additional revelations from Muhammad that Uthman did not find or approve of, and thus he failed to place them in his text....[89]

Early Alterations

From the above, it seems certain that even the *earliest* copies of the Quran must have contradicted one another or had other problems. Because these copies "led to such serious disputes between the faithful," it was necessary "to establish a text which should be the sole standard."[90] Dr. William Miller reveals that

> for some years after the death of Muhammad there was great confusion as to what material of all that had been preserved should be included in the Quran. Finally, in the caliphate of Uthman (644–656 A.D.) one text was given official approval, and all [other] material was destroyed.[91]

Muslim authority Alfred Guillaume further comments that "one of the secretaries he [Muhammad] employed boasted that he had induced the prophet to alter the wording of the revelations."[92]

Dr. Anis Shorrosh, a Christian Arab, concludes his own study of the Quran thus:

> It is not the Bible which is contradictory and confusing. No, it is definitely the Quran....No reasonable person presented with the evidence can believe otherwise.[93]

In conclusion, Muslims have never shown that the Bible has been corrupted. Nor have they shown that the Quran is an uncorrupted text. Rather, their position is accepted in the face of the evidence to the contrary.

CAN THE QURAN BE INTERPRETED OBJECTIVELY, AND WHY IS THIS IMPORTANT?

The interpretation of the Quran is critical because the Quran and Islamic law are what motivates Muslims and guides the Islamic world. Islamic society, how Muslims see their role in the wider world, and the interpretation of increasingly important topics like *jihad* are all based on the Quran and the application of Islamic law. (Islamic law is a separate matter, in that it did not derive directly from the Quran "but developed out of popular and administrative practice under the Ummayads," and has even departed from the Quran sometimes.)[94]

Muslims believe that only true believers can interpret the Quran properly, and also that Allah will give Muslims the proper interpretation. As one Muslim scholar says (seeking to overcome Muslims' reluctance to use translations),

> Quran was revealed in Arabic but God promised to be its teacher, 55:1-2, and the One to explain it, 75:19. God told us in 41:44 that language is irrelevant, and that only the sincere ones are going to understand the Quran irrespective of their language, while those who are not sincere or failed to worship Him ALONE will fail to understand it (even if they speak, read and write Arabic). See 56:79. Trust God and know that He is the teacher of the Quran.[95]

Clerics are usually the ones who interpret the Quran to the faithful. But for them, and for Muslims who read it themselves (many don't), the idea that Allah will supply the proper interpretation tends to foster a subjective approach to interpretation. This is illustrated in the historically broad differences in Quranic interpretation that have led to many contradictory views. Thus, one cleric may oppose the interpretation of another cleric. Radicals may claim that the interpretations of the moderate clerics are unjustified; some moderate clerics may oppose others on the basis that they lack real faith and "sincerity." In many ways, interpretation is completely up to the interpreter.

The Difficulty of Interpreting the Quran

Obviously, the interpretation of the Quran becomes a serious issue when it comes to vital topics that affect Islam or the rest of the world. Whose interpretation is right, and on what authority? Interpreting the Quran is not easy for many reasons, despite what some Muslims say.

Spending a few hours reading the Quran will show why; for example, lack of coherence and historical grounding in many places make contextual interpretation difficult. Commentaries help but do not solve the problem. Further, most Muslims do not even read the Quran; they rely upon the clerics to tell them what it means. One Muslim from Turkey expresses the feelings of many: "Now we are in Ramadan, I fast and practice, but I have never thought of reading the Quran, anyway I would not understand any of it. Even a Turkish version would not help."[96] Unfortunately, most clerics also don't know Arabic and must use a translation and commentaries, which vary widely in their interpretations of the sayings of Muhammad.

Another part of the problem for the clerics is that there are literally hundreds of thousands of *hadith*s that have influenced Islamic thinking. *Hadith*s are sayings of Muhammad from outside the Quran, and it is difficult to distinguish which are legitimate and which are illegitimate. These sayings have been examined in minute detail, but their interpretations of Islam differ and often cannot be reconciled. One Muslim scholar complains that within only 200 years after Muhammad, the situation was already out of hand.

> Two hundred years after hijra [Muhammad's exodus from Mecca to Medina], Bukhari collected a total of 600,000 hadiths. Out of these, he only verified 7,000 and rejected about 593,000 which he believed were false and not genuine. Other hadith scholars such as Muslim and Tarmizi accepted even less than the 7,000. There were hadiths accepted by Bukhari but rejected by other scholars who also

studied them, and vice versa. This happened only 200 years after hijra. After this, a lot of hadiths were created by other people....

In Islam's 1,400 years, they [Muslims] were exposed to a variety of teachings each claiming to be Islamic but which were opposites of each other. There were 1,001 beliefs ranging from narrow interpretations which rejected the present world outright and a desire to bring Islam back 1,400 years before, to one that alienated Islam and accepted secularism. As a result, the followers became very confused....[97]

None of this is to say that Islam does not agree on many fundamentals. The point is that Quranic interpretation has elasticity and subjective aspects that support a wide variety of "legitimate" interpretations. Many scholars agree that it can be easy for Muslims to become confused. Dr. J. Christy Wilson of Princeton points out that "some verses supersede and cancel others....Even to Muslims much of the text is unintelligible except through a commentary."[98]

Why So Many Problems?

In the introduction to his translation, Dawood comments that, because the Quran was originally written in the Kufic script and there was, therefore, no indication of vowels or diacritical points, "Variant readings are recognized by Muslims as of equal authority" and "it ought to be borne in mind that the Quran contains many statements which, if not recognized as altogether obscure, lend themselves to more than one interpretation."[99]

To add to the difficulty, in Sura 2:100 the Quran reads, "And for whatever verse We abrogate or cast into oblivion, We bring a better or the like of it; knowest thou not that God is powerful over everything?"[100] This verse may serve the Muslim as a rationale for contradictions between the Quran and the Bible or the Quran and itself, but nowhere in the Quran does Allah identify those verses he has apparently repealed.

In Sura 3:6 the Quran agrees that its ambiguous parts are incapable of interpretation, and only Allah knows their meaning.

> It is He who has revealed to you the Book. Some of its verses are precise in meaning—they are the foundation of the Book—and others ambiguous. Those whose hearts are infected with disbelief observe the ambiguous part, so as to create dissension by seeking to explain it. But no one knows its meaning except God. Those who are well grounded in knowledge say, "We believe in it; it is all from our Lord."[101]

We are told that the "precise" ("clear," per other translations) verses are the "foundation" ("essence" in other translations) of the Quran. If so, one could assume that Muslims would rarely disagree as to the interpretation of the clear parts. This is not what we find historically or today. Muslims have not identified which are the "precise" or "clear" parts and which are the "ambiguous" parts.

Further, how does the Muslim know all that is involved in having an "infected heart" or how this relates to knowing the location of the ambiguous parts? The Quran claims that "those who have been given the Book know it is the truth from their Lord...,"[102] and that it is a book whose "verses are made plain" (Sura 11:1); "a Book consistent" in its injunctions (39:23); and "expressed in clear language, wherein there is no deviation from the truth" (39:28). But how can a Muslim know these things?

Can Muslims Decide What Is Correct?
When critics charged Muhammad with tampering with the Quran, they themselves were charged with ignorance.

And when We exchange a verse in the place of another verse—and God knows very well what He is sending down—they say, "Thou art a mere forger!" Nay, but the most of them have no knowledge."[103]

Another translation reads, "When We change one verse for another (Allah knows best what He reveals), they say: 'You are an impostor.' Indeed, most of them are ignorant men."[104]

"Allah knows best what He reveals," but how are mortals to sort out the meaning? How does a Muslim decide which verse is "exchanged" or now preferred by Allah? Further, why would Allah exchange one verse in place of another verse? These are more than mere academic issues. Muslims trust in the Quran. But if Muslims are uncertain of what God says—and of His intention—how do they believe they can know God's will for their lives? How do they properly understand the role of Islam in the world?

The next two questions also illustrate the problem of the interpretation of the Quran—in regard to the treatment of women, and in regard to the issue of *jihad*.

WHAT DOES ISLAM TEACH ABOUT WOMEN?

The broadest context for an understanding of Islam's view of women can only be provided by examining the Quran and other sources of Islamic teaching, as we do below. Nonetheless, how women are treated in Islam today also depends on many other factors. One of the most important is the society in which they live—for example, women in Sudan or Algeria or Taliban-ruled Afghanistan live quite differently than Muslim women in America or Europe.

The background and temperament of the man a Muslim woman marries is also crucial, especially the extent to which he is involved in fundamentalist Islam. Moreover, if a Muslim man emphasizes the verses in the Quran that are positive towards women over those that are negative, and ignores the "negative Islamic culture" towards women in general, then the treatment he accords his wife (or wives) and other women will be substantially better than otherwise.

Islam as a whole often has a serious problem with how it treats women. Muslim clerics and other religious leaders are quite aware of this, and many of them have launched a major apologetic effort in order to present Islam's treatment of women favorably. As a group, however, women are fundamentally powerless within Islam (as indicated by, among other things, the small number and persecution of "women's rights" groups within Islam).

Sources of Teaching

The Quran contains some verses that speak of treating women fairly and kindly: "Consort with them [women] in kindness [ma'ruf]" (Sura 4:19; see also 30:21). Muhammad said, "I recommend that you treat women with goodness. The best of you are those who treat their wives the best." But even a review of all the verses in the Quran that contain the words "women" or "woman" will not reveal the true nature of Islamic treatment of women. This calls for an examination of the Hadith (the sayings of Muhammad)[105] and an examination of the application of Islamic law historically.[106]

Many of the citations we give below come from the older commentators, who are considered authoritative—even divinely authoritative.[107] While not all Muslim clerics use the older commentators or agree with them, many modern Islamic clerics do look to them for specific advice on applying Islam to society, family, law, and so on. Some Muslim leaders, even in the West, are calling for the practice of these teachings.

Below are some of the things Islam teaches about women in the Quran, the Hadith, and Islamic law.[108] Even many Muslims may be surprised by them. Taken together, these help explain why many Muslim women are mistreated despite Quranic injunctions to the contrary. (We should emphasize that the following material is not necessarily applicable to every Muslim or every Muslim nation, especially those influenced by the Western values that so many Muslims detest. We also encourage readers to carefully examine the Muslim response to charges that Islam is unfavorable toward women, for example, on the Internet.)

Teachings of Islamic Authorities

1. Men are, by creation, superior to women.

The Quran teaches, "Men are superior to women on account of the qualities with which God hath gifted the one above the other, and on account of the outlay they make from their substance for them..." (Sura 4:34). Ibn Kathir, the prominent commentator, said of this verse, "Men are superior to women, and a man is better than a woman."

> Even in our own time (1985) a Muslim writer, Ahmad Zaky Tuffaha, seriously and reverently quotes the following Hadith: "If a woman offered one of her breasts to be cooked and the other to be roasted, she still will fall short of fulfilling her obligations to her husband. And besides that if she disobeys her husband even for a twinkling of an eye, she would be thrown in the lowest part of Hell, except she repents and turns back."

2. Women are deficient in intelligence, religion, gratitude toward men and legal testimony.

> Razi, commenting on Q. [Quran] 4:11, said: "...Man is more perfect than the woman in creation, and intelligence, and in the religious sphere, such as the suitability to be a judge, and a leader in worship. Also, the testimony of the man is twice that of the woman [see also 2:282]....As the woman is deficient

in intelligence and of great lust, if she is given much money, much corruption will be the result."

...Commenting on the Quranic verse Q. 30:21, which states "And of His signs is that He created for you, of yourselves, spouses, that you may repose in them," Razi said: "...women are not charged with many commands as we are charged, because the woman is weak, silly, in one sense she is like a child, and no commands are laid upon a child...."

Women's lack of gratitude is expressed in another Hadith from Bukhari: "Women are ungrateful to their husbands and are ungrateful for the favours and the good (charitable) deeds done to them."

3. Women are sometimes described as animals or toys.

Eminent Muslim thinker Hadi Sabzevari...wrote: "That Sadr ad-Deen Shirazi classifies women as animals is a delicate allusion to the fact that women, due to the deficiency in their intelligence and understanding of intricacies, [etc.,]...are truly and justly among the mute animals."..."They have the nature of beasts,"..."but they have been given the disguise of human beings so that men would not be loath to talk to them...."

"Omar [one of the Khalifs] was once talking when his wife interjected, so he said to her: 'You are a toy, if you are needed we will call you.'"...And 'Amru Bin al-'Aas, also a Khalif, said: "Women are toys, so choose."

This was not just 'Amru Bin al-'Aas and Omar's opinions. Muhammad himself said, "'The woman is a toy, whoever takes her let him care for her (or "do not lose her").'"

4. Women are a thing to be ashamed of ('awrat), which is why they should veil their body and remain in the house as much as possible.

"The woman is 'awrah. When she goes outside (the house), the devil welcomes her." (This Hadith is classed as "Sahih," that is, "sound" or "faultless.") So going outside the house is a form of exposure of the 'awrah; a thing that delights the devil. This is why women are discouraged from going outside the house, even to pray in the mosque....Dr. Buti, a modern scholar,...gives the reason behind the wearing of the Hijab [veil]: "Allah, the most high, decreed that the woman should be veiled. He did so in protecting the chastity of the men who might see her, and not in protection of the chastity of the woman from the eyes of those who look at her."

5. The woman's obedience to the husband is her key to Paradise.

All the woman's piety is considered useless if she disobeys her husband. Her disobedience to her husband represents an unlawful and irrational act. But obedience to her husband is the key to Paradise, as is clear from the following Hadith: "...Whosoever female dies while her husband is pleased with her, will enter Paradise." "The prophet once said to a woman: 'Watch how you treat your husband for he is your Paradise and your Hell.'"

6. For disobedience, men are permitted to beat their wives.

Muhammad urged his followers to treat their wives well. He did not want to see them beaten without cause. He wanted good marriage relationships between husband and wife.[109]

The Quran teaches,

Men have authority over women because God has made the one superior to the other, and because they spend their wealth to maintain them. Good women are obedient. They guard their unseen parts because God has guarded them. As for those from whom you fear disobedience, admonish them and send them to beds apart and beat them. Then if they obey you, take no further action against them. Surely God is high, supreme (Sura 4:34).

Umar reported the prophet as saying: "A man will not be asked as to why he beat his wife."

The conclusion of one major study was as follows:

In review of the actual teachings of the Quran, Hadith, and Sira, Islam is rightly criticized....It will be shown from the Quran, Hadith, Sira, and other Islamic writings that this "Islamic" wife beating is physical and painful....You cannot separate the issue of wife beating apart from the context of her inferior position in the marriage relationship....

In Islam, the husband is the custodian of his wife. She is considered to be in-between slave and free. The woman is managed and controlled. The relationship between a married woman and her husband is similar to the relationship between parents and children....[110]

Rafiqul-Haqq and Newton comment, "The man who fears rebelliousness in his wife must admonish her first. If that does not work, the husband has the right to desert her sexually. If that does not work either, he has the right to beat her."

7. In the earthly life men are permitted multiple wives, and sexual rights to slave girls.

The Quran teaches,

> If ye fear that ye shall not be able to deal justly with
> the orphans, Marry women of your choice, Two or
> three or four; but if ye fear that ye shall not be able
> to deal justly [with multiple wives], then only one, or
> [a captive] that your right hands possess...(Sura 4:3).

Men have the right to have sex with their slave girls:

> If a man purchases a slave girl, the purchase con-
> tract includes his right to have sex with her....This
> contract is primarily to own her and secondarily to
> enjoy her sexually.
>
> The commentator Qortobi sees in that verse (Q.
> 4:3) that slave girls used as such by the free Muslim
> man "have neither sexual rights, nor financial rights."

**8. In Paradise, men will enjoy sex with perfect women
(perfect in beauty, and so on), but women are given no assurance of even one man in Paradise.**

> Another Hadith makes the number of wives sev-
> enty-two. Seventy females are specially created, and
> two are human females. His earthly wife may be
> included among his "huris," but in Paradise there
> will be additional women for him, even up to sev-
> enty-two.

After citing more examples, Rafiqul-Haqq and Newton
conclude,

> The above descriptions are literal, and the rela-
> tionship between men and their "huris" are phys-
> ical, and not only spiritual....Once again, the man
> has all the advantages and pleasures, while the
> woman must be perpetually used for his purposes.
> His is the pleasure—hers the disturbance, in this
> world and the next.

9. The woman's status lies somewhere between that of a "free" woman and a slave.

> Modern Muslims are not as straightforward as earlier commentators in admitting that the woman is the man's slave, but they agree the woman is inferior to the man....Women remain basically minors all their lives, and know nothing positive about the outside world and so few are ready to challenge the system.[111]

> The great Muslim scholar and philosopher Ghazali ...some seven hundred years ago,...summed up the situation, as follows: "The most satisfying and final word on the matter is that marriage is a form of slavery (riq). The woman is man's slave and her duty therefore is absolute obedience to the husband in all that he asks of her person."...The belief that the wife is the slave of the man is also shared by great scholars such as Razi and Ibn al-'Araby...by virtue of the payment of the dowry.

10. Divorce is the prerogative of the man.

Divorce is both abhorrent to Allah, and also lawful. The Hadith states,

> "The most detestable of lawful things near Allah is divorce."...The power to divorce usually resides in the hand of the man. Bukhari reported a Hadith that shows how easy the detestable and lawful act can be. A "man may say to his brother (in Islam), 'Have a look at either of my wives (and if you wish), I will divorce her for you.'"

Will Women Continue to be Mistreated Under Islam?

It appears that, to the degree Muhammad and Islamic history become the standard by which Muslim men treat their wives, Muslim women will continue to be mistreated. For example,

Muhammad received a revelation from God that a man should have no more than four wives at once, yet he himself had many more. He often mistreated his wives, and was apparently permitted the wives of other men. The Quran teaches the following:

> O Prophet! We have made lawful to thee thy wives to whom thou hast paid their dowers; and those whom thy right hand possesses out of the prisoners of war whom Allah has assigned to thee; and daughters of thy paternal uncles and aunts, and daughters of thy maternal uncles and aunts, who migrated [from Makka] with thee; and any believing woman who dedicates her soul to the Prophet if the Prophet wishes to wed her; this only for thee, and not for the Believers [at large]; We know what We have appointed for them as to their wives and the captives whom their right hands possess...(Sura 33:50).

Muhammad actually married a six- or seven-year-old named 'Aisha, and consummated the marriage when she was nine. Muslim authorities admit this, although they attempt to evade it. The Quran teaches that even Allah had to admonish the prophet:

> It is not lawful for thee ["to marry more"] women after this, nor to change them for ["other"] wives, even though their beauty attract thee, except any thy right hand should possess ["as handmaidens"]: and Allah doth watch over all things (33:52).

Even some Muslims admit to serious problems in the Muslim community's treatment of women. They also admit that little is done about it, which others think speaks volumes about Islam's view of women. For example:

> Wife abuse has hurt many Muslim women, destroyed many Muslim families, and weakened the entire Muslim community....How much more abuse will Muslim women have to endure before the community decides that enough is enough?[112]

21

WHY DO MUSLIMS HAVE DIFFERENT VIEWS ABOUT WAR (JIHAD) AND PEACE, AND HOW DOES THIS RELATE TO TERRORISM?

Part of the difficulty in addressing Islamic views on important subjects like peace or war lies in the interpretation of the Quran and the vast body of regulations in the *sharia*. When we look at Islam historically or today, we discover contradictory teachings on various issues not only among Muslims but in the Quran and *sharia* themselves. This makes it difficult to ascertain what the "right" or "true" interpretation in application to a particular subject might be. Radicals who claim to speak for Islam, unlike its moderate clerics, dismiss lengthy study of the millenium of Muslim debate among jurists, theologians, and scholars in favor of what, to them, are clear and simple verses in the Quran that support their interests.

There are teachings in the Quran that emphasize that Islam is to be a religion of goodness and peace, one that respects non-Muslims as creations of Allah. At least one verse declares there is to be no compulsion in religion (Sura 2:256). On the other hand, there are teachings in the Quran that speak rather negatively of Christians, Jews, polytheists, and other "unbelievers," or "infidels." These can be used to justify persecution of these people as Allah's will (see questions 22 and 31). To illustrate the different views one can find, consider the following verses:

> Strongest among men in enmity to the believers wilt thou find the Jews and Pagans; and nearest among them in love to the believers wilt thou find those who say, "We are Christians": because amongst these are men devoted to learning and men who have renounced the world, and they are not arrogant (5:82).

Here, among all people, Jews and pagans are described as being the most hostile to Muslims. This has not tended to help Jewish–Muslim relations or the relationship among Muslims and polytheists, such as Hindus. Christians, however, are given the favor of Allah because they have shown love to Muslims and because among them are the learned.

On the other hand, in the same chapter the Quran also teaches that Muslims must avoid Christians because they are corrupt, unjust, and cursed of God.

> O ye who believe! Take not the Jews and the Christians for your friends and protectors: They are but friends and protectors to each other. And he amongst you that turns to them [for friendship] is of them. Verily Allah guideth not a people unjust (5:51).

And,

> The Jews call 'Uzair a son of Allah, and the Christians call Christ the son of Allah. That is a saying from their mouth; [in this] they but imitate what the unbelievers of old used to say. Allah's curse be on them: how they are deluded away from the Truth! (9:30).

This underscores a genuine problem in Islam. Many Quranic verses cannot be logically placed into any historical context; and the entire text, as the eternal word of God, is said to be above history. So how do Muslims determine their approach to the Christian community? Muslims can find justification for their personal beliefs even when those beliefs are contradictory to those of other Muslims. Indeed, both Muslim radicals and Islamic moderates can find the same divine sanction for their varying beliefs and actions. To give an illustration dealing with a serious issue, what the British government officially identified as Islamic terror organizations were identified by the *Muslim News* (on-line) as "Muslim liberation movements." They can't be both.[113]

The Contemporary Problem

How does this problem of contradiction relate to the twenty-first century? The difficulty for moderate Islam is that its theological and legal authorities cannot prove that fundamentalist and radical Islam is *not* Islamic, because these forms of Islam are also supported by the Quran. For example, Osama bin Laden believed that the Quran justified his terrorist acts because he quoted the Quran in support of terrorism in his *fatwa*s (legal rulings with religious authority). Radical Muslim clerics, who want to see Islam engaged in a protracted war against its enemies, have done the same. Islam needs to determine how, specifically, it can deal with this far-reaching conundrum. If it doesn't, the only question is which form of Islam will win out in the future.

As we will see in question 31, classical Islam, while strictly regulating military *jihad* through rules as to engagement and resolution, nonetheless did use *jihad* militarily to expand Islam, since, as was believed, Islam was the world's only opportunity for peace. The following analysis shows the difference between classical Islam and most of today's Islam in the interpretation of *jihad*.

> John Kelsay [in *Islam and War,* 1993] offers us this description of the classical Islamic teaching regarding war: "The territory of Islam is theoretically the territory of peace and justice....Islam provides the best and most secure peace available to humanity. The peace of the world cannot be fully secure unless all people come under the protection of an Islamic state. Thus there always exists an imperative for Muslims: to struggle to extend the boundaries of the territory of Islam....The struggle to extend the boundaries of the territory of Islam is the jihad" (page 34).

Before the advent of Islam, Arab tribes fought each other. Now that they embraced the new faith and have become brothers, they were no longer to raid and plunder each other. Their energies had to be spent in the territories of the Infidel. Following the death of Muhammad in 632 A.D., his successors, the caliphs, presided over the conquest of the world. By 732, the Arab Muslim empire extended from Spain to India. Theorizing on the subject of war among Muslims followed their conquests. The lands belonging to them were known as Darul-Islam (Household of Islam) and the lands outside that realm were designated as Darul-Harb (Household of War.)

"Since in Islam there is no distinction between 'church' and state, religion and politics, the faith may be spread by preaching or by war: [For Sunni intellectuals,] 'normal' war is connected with the effort to extend the boundaries of Islamic territory. This struggle, for which the preferred means is the spread of the Islamic message through preaching, teaching, and the like, may nevertheless take on the character of war....The territory of Islam—really, the world—could not be a secure place until and unless Islamic hegemony was acknowledged everywhere. To secure such hegemony was the goal of the jihad, or 'struggle in the path of God.' According to Sunni theorists, war or jihad by means of killing is justified when a people resists or otherwise stands in opposition to the legitimate goals of Islam" (page 61).

But what about today's Muslim thinkers? On the one hand, they realize that to live in our modern world, they cannot simply hold on to the classical Islamic view regarding the legitimacy of war as a means for the expansion of the faith. They can quote the Quranic verse "There is no compulsion in religion" (2:256) to support some type of

modus vivendi with peoples and nations living
outside Darul-Islam.[114]

Given the increasing influence of Islamic fundamentalism,
the question here is, What happens if Islam moves further
toward the classical interpretation? As noted above, Muslims
often cite Sura 2:256 in defense of themselves: "There is no
compulsion in religion—the right way is indeed clearly distinct from error...." But if there is a problem of how to interpret the Quran accurately, then verses cited by those seeking to
reinterpret or limit *jihad* are unlikely to remain a secure bul-
wark against classical interpretations or radical terrorism.
Quoting verses like Sura 2:256 does not appear to be working
even today, at least not everywhere, as we will now illustrate.

22

IS ISLAM A TOLERANT RELIGION?

The translator's preface to one English translation of the
Quran emphasizes that Islam is a religion that is more than tolerant: "Tolerance is not, in fact, the word that can sufficiently
indicate the breadth of the attitude of Islam toward other religions. It preaches equal love for all, equal respect for all, and
equal faith in all."[115] And in his commentary on Sura 22:40, this
translator remarks, "The religious freedom which was established by Islam thirteen hundred years ago has not yet been surpassed by the most civilized and tolerant of nations."[116]

One wishes this were true. One hopes that most Muslims,
especially in America, are tolerant of other faiths. However,
considered globally, the legislative application of Islam is often
another matter. When a Muslim state is not "secular" (Turkey
is the only "secular" Islamic state) but has universally applied
Islamic law to the nation, life can become difficult for non-
Muslims. Whatever good exists in Islam, when we look at the
world scene, tolerance for other religions does not appear to be

one of its stronger points, at least as far as Islamic governments are concerned. (In the material below, it should be noted that Islamic discrimination and aggression has more often been instituted by Islamic rulers, or by radical Muslims, than by "average" Muslims.)

Human Rights Under Islam

Westerners need to understand that Muslim nations in general have no concept of "separation of church and state," and that even in moderate or "secular" states, Islamic law can still be applied forcefully, even fully, as in Saudi Arabia. Church and state are one, and the religion of Islam, through *sharia*, or Islamic law, dominates all aspects of society. Thus, there are no independent "human rights" as recognized in the West; all individual rights are subject to the priorities of Islamic law. Islam, as the state religion, requires that everything be subject to it.

This is why Islamic nations have revised universal declarations of human rights and have substituted their own declarations of human rights predicated upon the truth of Islam.

> The concepts of human rights and democracy are alien to Islam. Even though most Islamic countries signed the Universal Declaration of Human Rights when it was first promulgated in 1948, many have since then hedged their bets and have qualified their support by signing, for example, the so-called Universal Islamic Declaration of Human Rights. This later document accepts human rights "insofar as they conform to Islamic law," which is not very far.[117]

> Article 24 of the 1990 Cairo Declaration of Human Rights, for example, states that "All rights and freedoms mentioned in this statement are subject to the Islamic Sharia," and Article 25 adds, "The Islamic Sharia is the only source for the interpretation or explanation of each individual article of this statement."

> ...In the Islamic states, Islam is the state religion, to which all citizens are assumed to belong, and which is considered to be the "stabilizing principle. The State is bearer of a religious idea and is, therefore, itself a religious institution. It is responsible for the worship of God, for religious training and for the spreading of the faith."[118]

As a result, Muslim nations typically give Muslims full legal rights, and non-Muslims few legal rights. Since Islam is the primary stabilizing factor of society and is the will of Allah, Muslims are the maintainers of social stability and the divine order. Non-Muslims are those who ignore (or oppose) social stability and divine order. This is why there are such severe penalties for Muslims who leave their faith and convert to another religion, or for non-Muslims who participate in the process: The social and divine order has been threatened. Martin Forstner concludes, "Only he who believes in God and the divinely revealed Quran, and who obeys the Sharia, is able to become a competent citizen, whereas the ungodly are enemies of society."[119]

Thus, Christians are not permitted to share their faith in Muslim countries without penalty, even sometimes the death penalty, while Muslims are free to share their faith with anyone.

> It is forbidden for non-Moslems to insult or disparage Islam, the Quran or the prophet Mohammed, which automatically occurs in Christian evangelisation, according to Moslem opinion. Moroccan law, for example, requires a prison sentence of six months to three years, as well as a fine of 200 to 500 dirham, for proselytizing a Moslem to another religion. Repudiation of Islam is still considered to be a crime worthy of death, whereas the Moslem has the right to proselytize others.[120]

Persecution Under Islam

If Islam is as tolerant of other religions as Muslims frequently claim, we would like to know why it has so harshly, even brutally, persecuted Christians? Such persecution has occurred in even moderate states like Saudi Arabia—which, according to one watchdog list, has been the worst offender more than once. "Moderate" Saudi Arabia illustrates "...the Prophet's famous saying: 'Two religions shall not remain together in the peninsula of the Arabs.'" This has meant that, to this day, the establishment of any other religion in Saudi Arabia is forbidden. Thus Christianity and other religions have been marginalized and persecuted. Saudi Arabia's endorsement of one "purist" branch of Islam, Wahhabism, and the Saudi exporting of it far and wide, may go far in explaining its persecution of Christians, but it can hardly justify it.

In the year 2000, the Christian information organization Open Doors published its Top Ten List of the "worst persecutors of Christians." Seven of the 10 worst offenders were Muslim nations, Saudi Arabia being first. In 1999, 15 of the top 20 worst offenders were Muslim nations.[121] In a 1998 study, 42 countries were listed as engaging in the persecution of Christians, and at least 25 of these were Muslim.[122] (To give another indication, there are now at least a dozen Web sites devoted to Islamic persecution of Christians.) What happened to Muslim tolerance of other religions?

If Arab and Muslim governments allegedly have great concern over the plight of "oppressed" peoples like the Palestinians, how can they ignore the terrible plight and persecution of Christians, or actually participate in the persecution of Christians? For instance, over the past years some 2 million black Christians have been slaughtered in Islamic-dominated Sudan, and millions more may be targeted for destruction. Where is official Islamic concern for them?

An interview with Islamic authority Anthony J. Dennis, the author of *The Rise of the Islamic Empire and the Threat to the West,* illustrates this point:

> The fundamentalist Muslims advocate and practice
> on a huge scale the systematic torture, persecution,

imprisonment and even execution of non-Muslim groups, especially Baha'is and Christians. It's a capital offense to convert voluntarily from Islam to Christianity in Iran and other places, or even to translate the Bible into Farsi in Iran. And of course, the Sudanese government, which is a close ally with Iran and is staunchly fundamentalist, has practiced the enslavement of Christian children and the forcible conversion of their parents, with torture and death awaiting those who don't convert. What has gone on in terms of human rights abuses inside these countries is truly mind-boggling. And these governments make no bones about it. They go right on handing out death sentences for political opponents or Christian believers in Iran who don't convert or stop their proselytizing.[123]

Why the Fear?

One wonders, what do Muslims have to fear from Christians? Their good behavior? What they fear, unfortunately, is Christianity itself and its threat to the influence or expansion of Islam. Muslims fear Christianity because, in their eyes, Christian faith has led some 2 billion people to reject Allah for a false god and has thereby prevented the expansion of Islam in a most important way. An important article at SecularIslam.org shows that Muslims who do not want religious tolerance have little trouble justifying their reason to fear Christianity:

> ...Between two or three million Muslims converted to Christianity after the massacres of the communists in Indonesia in 1965....In France alone, in the 1990s, there are two or three hundred converts to Christianity from Islam, each year. According to Ann Mayer, in Egypt conversions have been "occurring with enough frequency to anger Muslim clerics and to mobilize conservative Muslim

opinion behind proposals to enact a law imposing the death penalty for apostasy...."

Those who convert to Christianity and choose to stay in the Muslim country do so at great personal danger. The convert has most of his rights denied him, identity papers are often refused him, so that he has difficulties leaving his country; his marriage is declared null and void, his children are taken away from him to be brought up by Muslims, and he forfeits his rights of inheritance. Often the family will take matters into their own hands and simply assassinate the apostate; the family are, of course, not punished....[124]

Apologists of Islam still insist on perpetuating the myth of an Islam which accorded equality to her non-Muslim subjects....The same apologists minimize, or even excuse, the persecution, the discrimination, the forced conversions, the massacres, the destruction of the churches, synagogues, fire temples and other places of worship....[125]

Moderate Muslim nations have the power to stop these atrocities, but still they choose not to.

In conclusion, when Islamic nations who claim to honor Allah—and to honor His respect for His creation—band together to end the cruel persecution of Christians and other religious minorities in Muslim states, then we will happily acknowledge the Islamic tolerance of others who disagree with them.

23

IN WHAT SENSE IS ISLAM A RELIGION OF PEACE?

And the servants of (Allah) Most Gracious are those who walk on the earth in humility and when the ignorant address them, they say, "Peace!" (Sura 25:63).

Be not weary and faint-hearted, crying for peace, when ye should be uppermost: for Allah is with you, and will never put you in loss for your [good] deeds (47:35).

Some people wonder, "If Islam is a 'religion of peace,' how could an event of the magnitude of the September 11 attack ever happen?" Many argue that Islam *is* a peaceful religion, but in which happens to reside a minority of very violent radicals. As one Iranian fundamentalist scholar argues, "Religion must of course advocate peace, and the Quran says…'Peace is better,' but it must also advocate war."[126]

Many Muslims emphasize the peaceful nature of their religion, and certainly, Muslims individually strive for inward peace, and also peace with their neighbors. Islam as a religion has had periods of peace throughout its history. But there seems to be a long way to go for Islam to realize its stated ideals. (Again, as we look at the material below, it needs to be emphasized that Islamic aggression has often been instigated by Islamic rulers or by radical Muslims, not by average Muslims, who are often its victims also.)

Islam's Tendency Toward War

There exists in Islam a divine sanction—even encouragement—for war that individual peace-oriented Muslims have not been able to successfully countermand. To some, Muslim history seems almost as much occupied with warfare as with peaceful coexistence. As one group of secular Muslims points out, from the seventh to the fourteenth centuries, Islam "is riddled with violence, fratricide, and wars of aggression…."[127] The first century of Islam was one long conquest of Arabia and beyond. In the time of the Crusades, Islam was the initial aggressor, with Christianity responding defensively. In the twentieth century, we saw Iraq attack Kuwait, causing large

Muslim casualties (and leading to the Gulf War). We also saw Shiite Iran attack Sunni Iraq, with more than 1 million Muslims dying in the ensuing conflict. And in the present century, Iran gave the U.S. grudging support in its war against terrorism not because Iranian Muslims love America so much, but because they hate the Muslim Taliban of Afghanistan so thoroughly.

Another factor in Islam's tendency toward conflict is the existence of certain aggressive branches or schools. For instance, the Saudi regime has encouraged a form of fundamentalist reform Islam that many other Muslims hate. But the regime, along with the Muslim Brethren, has exported far and wide this brand of Islam that is susceptible to radicalism. The history of this movement known as *al-Muwahhidun* ("Wahhabism" to their enemies) over the last 250 years involves many conflicts between Muslims.

What Does the Quran Say?

With a history of such conflict, how then can Islam be considered a "religion of peace"? Many Muslims emphasize inner emotional peace and peace with Allah; or they point to the ultimate outcome of Islam, which will finally bring peace to the world. Once Islam is dominant globally by peaceful means, then peace will rule the world, they say, basing this in doctrines they find in the Quran.

However the attitude and actions of other Muslims are also based on the Quran, which teaches that Islam is to fight against unbelievers until all false religion is vanquished. Though some see this as metaphorically occurring through peaceful proselytizing, many others hold to more forceful methods. While we will discuss the issue of *jihad* in more detail later (see question 31), for now we will briefly illustrate that *jihad* does present some severe problems for an Islam that claims to be a peaceful religion. Consider these statements by what appear to be moderate Muslims.

Allaah, the Most High and the Most Majestic, has stated the objectives behind jihaad in the cause of Allaah, the Most High. He, the Most Perfect, says: "Fight them until there is no more fitnah (shirk [false religion]), and the religion will be for Allaah Alone. But if they cease (worshipping others besides Allaah) then certainly Allaah is All-Seer of what they do [words of Soorah al-Anfaal]."[128]

Since lawful warfare is essentially jihad and since its aim is that the [that is, all] religion is God's entirely [2:189, 8:39] and God's word is uppermost [9:40], therefore, according to all Muslims, those who stand in the way of this aim must be fought....[129]

Sayyid Mujtaba Musavi Lari also points out in "The Jehad—The Holy War" that Islam brings peace to the world through its expansion, and that this does not happen without warfare. Those who oppose peace will fight Islam and so must be fought by Islam.

As a world faith for everyone everywhere, Islam knows no geography; but must extend to every last soul in every last region of the world....History shows that no established order was ever replaced by a new superior order without some warfare....Islam [will] run into opposition from people with vested interests in corruption....

Islam does not war against people. It wars against oppression....Islam's aim is that the knowledge of God should cover the earth as the waters cover the sea...and to this end Muslims are prepared to give their lives in peace or if necessary, in war....

In his book entitled "War and Peace in Islam," Dr. Majid Khadouri writes,... "[Islam's] first success was in uniting the nations which accepted it within themselves, so that civil wars ceased. It went on to found a family of Islamic nations at peace with each other. It aims to bring that blessing to the whole world. Thus the aim of the Jehad is peace on earth, and that will be its final result."[130]

In other words, once everyone agrees that Islam is the truth, by whatever means of persuasion, then the world will be peaceful. Some Muslims think the problem is all the unbelievers who try to "destroy" and "annihilate" Islam by rejecting or opposing its beliefs—like Christians and adherents of other religions. As another Muslim source declares, citing the Quran (Sura 4:144):

> Islam is the religion of peace and harmony for all mankind. It was Islam that brought light in darkness. But the disbelievers have always tried to destroy Muslims and Islam. In Quran Allah says: "O Ye who believe! Take not for friends unbelievers rather than believers. Do ye wish to offer Allah an open proof against yourselves?"[131]

Conflict Under Islam

We look out across the world and what we see is not encouraging for either believers or unbelievers, with many recent and contemporary wars all involving Islam in some way. For instance, the Afghan civil war was begun by the Islamic Taliban sect (influenced by Wahhabism) and has involved thousands of casualties among Muslims. The Islamic Palestine Liberation Organization (PLO) has a master plan to destroy Israel in the name of Allah, which has brought Arabs and Jews into perpetually simmering warfare. Moderate Muslim governments are subject to subversion and terrorist attacks by Muslim radicals. There is the continuing war between Muslim Pakistan and Hindu India in the Kashmir that has resulted in tens of thousands of dead Hindus and who knows how many dead Muslims. Indeed, some 5 to 7 million people, including many

Muslims, have been killed in Islamic-related wars in the last 30 years. On the larger scene, the conflict between Iraq and the West is ongoing.

Consider in brief just a few more instances of conflict.

- heavy fighting in Algeria between Islamic fundamentalists and the military
- war between Christian Ethiopia and Muslim Eritrea
- conflict in Kosovo between the Christian Serbs and the Muslim Albanians
- the ongoing hostility between Turkey and Greece
- the Islamic Party of Kenya's declaration of *jihad* on the government
- Nigeria's civil war between Muslims and Christians
- war in Chechnya and Daghestan, both Muslim areas in the Caucasus
- Muslim insurrection against the pro-Russian regimes in Tajikistan and Uzbekistan in Central Asia

Muslims in various other places are either fomenting insurrection or instigating conflicts by their policies toward non-Muslims. For example—

- the Chinese-Islamic war involving Uighur Muslims in East Turkestan (more usually known as Sinkiang Province) in Western China
- the ongoing war in the southern Philippines between Catholics and Muslims
- conflict, indeed genocide, in East Timor in Indonesia, where Christians are demanding independence to preserve their beliefs

Why so much conflict involving Islam? As we will see later, what Muslims view as a defensive *jihad* can actually involve offensive military action, for instance, preemptive strikes to protect Islam from perceived aggression. Or those Muslim rulers who wish to justify military aggression may claim to "liberate" what they call "oppressed" peoples. The problem is interpretive. Consider this verse from the Quran: "Permission to fight is given to those upon whom war is made because they are oppressed..." (Sura 22:39). This could refer to Muslims under attack—or this and other verses could be used to justify fighting to "liberate" Muslims, such as, for example, those "oppressed" by an "uprising" of Sudanese Christians. These Christians are accused of making "war" on Islam, but they really only want to be left alone to practice their faith without discrimination or persecution.

And in this vein was the vicious September 11 attack on America by Muslim radicals, which brought great reproach to Islam and brought many to even hate the Muslim religion. One solemn cartoon captured the issue. It showed a jet plane labeled "Islamic terrorists" about to smash into a towering book labeled "The Holy Koran." Millions of Westerners now view Islam's holy book as dead and buried, with "September 11" its unholy epitaph.

All this must bring great pain and difficulty to Muslims who desire peace. Islam clearly has some work to do, and Muslims who care about peace must not only reform Islam, they must proactively oppose radical Islam. Moreover, current Islamic governments are characterized by repression. Is this what modern Muslims want?

In conclusion, Islam has far to travel before it becomes the "religion of peace" that many Muslims desire. Indeed, the current issues and problems surrounding Islam (as seen, for example, in the lengthy articles at the Web site Secular-Islam.org) are not at all encouraging for the future of Islam, especially when we take into account what is documented concerning Islam's past. But there is still hope. Islam may have within it the power to change. The question is, will it?

SECTION V

THE CONNECTION BETWEEN ISLAM AND TERRORISM

24

WHAT CAN WE LEARN ABOUT ISLAM FROM THE EXAMPLE OF OSAMA BIN LADEN?

Osama bin Laden and the radical Muslim Taliban, along with the global terrorist al-Qaeda organization, were the masterminds behind the September 11 attack on the United States. Bin Laden was responsible for the murder of more than 5,000 innocent Americans. He was also the one most responsible for putting the terrorist Taliban sect into power in Afghanistan.

It is important to understand bin Laden's beliefs, because there are thousands of radical Muslims who believe the same things as he does. (Already he is a great martyr of Islam in the minds of millions of Muslims.) Here are some observations about him that will shed light on the thinking of many, if not most, radicals.

- Bin Laden became a hero, not just to the radicals, but to literally millions of Muslims. According to an article in the *Los Angeles Times*, "He [bin Laden] is already the most popular political figure in the Islamic world: Usama is the second most popular name, after Mohammed, for male children there."[132]

- Bin Laden's philosophy teaches these same Muslim children to relish the idea of becoming murderers (see question 25). In a 1996 *fatwa* (religious command), he said, "Youths want only one thing, to kill you so they can go to paradise." In special training schools around the world, thousands of children are taught to die—and they really wish to die—in the cause of Allah.

- Bin Laden was never a social reformer—despite his claims, he cares little for the plight of, for example, the Palestinians. (Indeed, the Arab Muslim world hardly gave them a glance either until they found they could use them as pawns for their own purposes. Research of the history of the Palestinians reveals this.)

- Bin Laden came to believe that not just Israel, but America and the West generally, represented a great threat to Islam. He also came to believe that moderate Muslim nations were in fact betrayers of true Islam.

  For instance, when Saudi Arabia permitted American troops on its soil during the Gulf War, bin Laden became outraged that the Muslim holy lands had become "defiled" and that evil "infidels" had been permitted to war against other Muslims (the people of Iraq). Thus, in a 1999 interview he said, "Muslim scholars have issued a fatwa [a religious order] against any American who pays taxes to his government. He is our target, because he is helping the American war machine against the Muslim nation."[133]

  And as *Newsweek* reported on September 24, 2001, "Osama bin Laden thanked almighty Allah and bowed before him when he heard the news [of the successful 9/11 attack]."

Origins of Radicalism

But what really made bin Laden and those like him? What created their worldview, their hatred? They have all kinds of complaints about the "unjust," "apostate," "murderous" moderate Muslim regimes who have, in their view, oppressed their people, compromised with the West, perverted their faith, and prevented true Islamic peace and justice from expanding globally. They believe that, somehow, America has mercilessly slaughtered Muslims by the thousands. Further, they believe that the Jews have stolen Muslim lands that Allah and the Quran have promised to Arabs—and it is America's power that keeps these lands stolen.

For purposes of argument, let's assume all the above is true—but how does this possibly justify what bin Laden and those like him have done? What brought about the veneration of such bloodthirsty acts and ideals within much of Islam?

There is one good possibility to explain their rage—the inflammatory verses of the Quran. (One can only wonder if these Muslim radicals would have become terrorists without the Quran.) Most Muslims aren't terrorists, but their holy book still seems to be what nurtures the anger, ignites the rage, and turns those like bin Laden to terrorism. What the Quran has promised Arabs; what Allah says about the Jew or Christian, the infidel or Muslim apostate, the superiority of believer over unbeliever, the final victory of Islam over the world; the *jihad* verses; the ease of interpreting the Quran to justify personal whim—all these and more seem extremely relevant to the making of Islamic terrorists.

Social commentator William Buckley put it this way:

> Carefully selected, there are Quranic preachments that are consistent with civilized life. But on September 11th we were looked in the face by a deed done by Muslims who understood themselves to be acting out Muslim ideals. It is all very well for individual Muslim spokesmen to assert the misjudgment of the terrorist, but the Islamic world is substantially made up of countries that ignore, or countenance, or support terrorist activity. Mustafa Kamal Uddin, a 32-year-old body-and-fender man in Karachi, explained it to a New York Times reporter. "You see," he said, "holy wars come about only when Allah has no other way to maintain justice, times like now. That is why Allah took out his sword" on September 11th.

We demand to know: Who taught Mustafa Kamal Uddin to reason in that way, and the crowds in Karachi to support such thinking? [Here there was a photo of mobs in Karachi, Pakistan, denouncing the U.S. and carrying signs reading "CRUSH AMERICA."].... Either restore the proper Allah—or get ready for a holy war.[134]

If we look at the Quran, we can see terrorists such as bin Laden both condemned and justified. On the one hand, they stand condemned: "If you desire to exact retribution, then adjust the penalty to the wrong you have suffered" (Sura 16:127). And, "Allah enjoins justice and benevolence, and graciousness as between kindred, and forbids evil designs, ill behavior and transgression. He admonishes you that you may take heed" (16:91). On the other hand, they can also justify their actions by how they interpret the above verses, or others like these: "Do not destroy life that Allah has made sacred, save for just cause" (17:33). "Slay not the soul which Allah has forbidden, except in the cause of justice" (25:68). "You shall not kill—for that is forbidden by God—except for a just cause" (6:152).

A Terrorist's View

The terrorists' cause is just, at least in their own minds. Whatever made men such as bin Laden, his breed are here to stay, and it is best that we know as much as possible about them. One of their outstanding characteristics is irrational hatred of America, Israel, and Muslim governments they deem apostate—but especially America. Here, for example, are some of bin Laden's declarations, from a 1999 interview.

[Answering questions from his followers] "[T]errorizing [American, Western, Muslim apostate] oppressors and criminals and thieves and robbers is necessary for the safety of people and for the protection of their property....The terrorism we practice is of the commendable kind, for it is directed at the tyrants and the aggressors and the enemies of Allah, the tyrants, the traitors who commit acts of treason against their own countries and their own faith and their own prophet and their own nation....America heads the list of aggressors against Muslims....

[Answering questions from reporter John Miller] Allah has created us for the purpose of worshipping him. He is the one who has created us and who has favored us with this religion. Allah has ordered us to make holy wars and to fight to see to it that His word is the highest and the uppermost and that of the unbelievers the lowermost....We do not care what the Americans believe. What we care for is to please Allah....We believe that the worst thieves in the world today and the worst terrorists are the Americans....We do not have to differentiate between military or civilian. As far as we are concerned, they are all targets.

I am one of the servants of Allah and I obey his orders. Among those is the order to fight for the word of Allah...and to fight until the Americans are driven out of all the Islamic countries....We are certain—with the grace of Allah—that we shall prevail over the Jews and over those fighting with them....Americans have committed unprecedented stupidity. They have attacked Islam and its most significant sacrosanct symbols....They shall all be wiped out....[135]

Bin Laden's words, unfortunately, illustrate the attitude of thousands of radical Muslims around the world—that America, Israel, and even Muslim nations that help America are the supreme enemies of God (Allah), the Quran, and all true Muslims. We must take all this into account when thinking about Islam and dealing with its followers.

Why and How Do Some Radical Muslims Teach Their Children to Kill Americans?

As I (Weldon) write, I am looking at a color picture of what must be a five-year-old boy, with a hate-filled grimace, submachine gun in hand, striking a typical terrorist pose. The radicals are so full of hate that they even teach their own children to abhor and kill Americans. Why? Because America is the great enemy who has harmed Islam by protecting Zionist Israel, supporting "corrupt" Arab and Muslim governments, and bringing corrupt Western values and immorality to Muslim lands.

It is one thing for evil adults to choose to become terrorists or to support them. It is quite another for those same adults to train and indoctrinate innocent children to become murderers—killers even of civilians, of women and children. We can only be reminded of the severe warning of Jesus about the fate of those who cause such little ones to stumble (Matt. 18:6). (On the other hand, if even respected Arab newspapers teach hate, why should we be surprised about the radicals? The official Egyptian daily, *Al-Akbar,* had these words: "Kill your enemies at every turn because this is a life and death conflict between you and them."[136])

If we become aware of what happens in thousands of radical Muslim religious schools around the world, we will better understand Islamic terrorism (and the September 11 attacks). These schools teach children to hate America and to murder Americans. One day these children will grow up, and the world will have to deal with their training in more direct ways. According to *USA Today,* Pakistan alone (population, 140 million) has an estimated 40,000 *madrassas* (Muslim religious schools). Of these, the government estimates that six to seven thousand are militant. (It is estimated that there are 6 to 20 million radical Muslims in that nation.) The militant schools may have hundreds of thousands of students—and these estimates may be low. The schools are supported by wealthy Muslims from around the world. The students spend up to six hours a day memorizing the Quran, and two to four hours per day listening to lectures about the Quran and Islam.

As a *USA Today* article reports, the schools begin the day with a prayer: Thousands of students say, in unison, "O Allah, defeat the enemies of Muslims and make Islam and the Taliban victorious over the Americans in Afghanistan." Then they break into a chorus of *"Jihad! Jihad!"* or "Holy war! Holy war!" "We are all Osama bin Ladens," says a senior teacher at one *madrassa*. The chancellor of another school declares, "I, and all my students, will support the Taliban and Osama at all costs. They are the only ones implementing true Islam."[137]

The *USA Today* article goes to say that the Muslim radicals who teach at these schools are convinced that America is not engaged in a war against terror, but a war against Islam. At yet another *madrassa*, a student who attended a bin Laden training camp pulled out his training manual, called the "Encyclopedia" (which is used at terrorist training camps in Afghanistan).

> "Now listen, American, and listen well," he says. He reads from page 12: "'Bomb their embassies and vital economic centers.' That's what I will do to you and your country. I will get your children. I will get their playgrounds. I will get their schools, too. I will get all of you." Another student promises he will "kill more than [Muhammad] Atta," the apparent mastermind of the September 11 hijackers who flew into the South Tower. Another holds up a picture of the Sears Tower in Chicago. "This one is mine," he promises.[138]

WHY DO SUICIDE TERRORISTS BELIEVE THEIR ACTS WILL TAKE THEM TO HEAVEN?

Radical Muslims have been taught by their clerics that death in the cause of Allah will guarantee them Paradise. They can also see such teaching in the Quran. For example,

> Let those then fight in the cause of Allah who would exchange the present life with the Hereafter. Whoso fights in the cause of Allah, be he slain, or be he victorious, We shall soon give him a great reward.... Those who believe fight in the cause of Allah, and those who disbelieve fight in the cause of the Evil One. Fight ye then against the friends of Satan (Sura 4:75-77).

> Allah will never render vain the works of those who are slain in His cause. He will guide them and improve their condition, and admit them into the Garden which he has made known to them (47:4-5).

The Quran contains many descriptions of the blissful nature of the afterlife, for example,

> The dutiful will be surely in Gardens and Bliss.... Eat and drink with pleasure for what you did, reclining on thrones set in lines, and We shall join them to pure, beautiful ones [virgins],...and We shall aid them with fruit and flesh, as they desire (52:17,19-20,22).

The radicals make the most of verses like these in order to attain their personal terrorist goals. They also promise martyrs that their families will be cared for because of their commitment to Allah. For example, in his first *fatwa*, Osama bin Laden taught the following, citing several verses from the Quran:

These youths [young martyrs] love death as you [Americans] love life....These youths believe in what has been told by Allah and His messenger....about the greatness of the reward for the Mujahideen and Martyrs; Allah, the most exalted, said: "And [so far as] those who are slain in the way of Allah, He will by no means allow their deeds to perish. He will guide them and improve their condition. And cause them to enter the garden [paradise] which He has made known to them." (Muhammad; 47:4-6)...

He also said: "[to] a martyr privileges are guaranteed by Allah; forgiveness with the first gush of his blood, he will be shown his seat in paradise, he will be decorated with the jewels of belief (Imaan), married off to the beautiful ones, protected from the test in the grave, assured security in the day of judgement,... wedded to seventy-two of the pure Houries (beautiful ones of Paradise) and his intercession on the behalf of seventy of his relatives will be accepted...."[139]

The Teachings for an Attack

The teachings given to the 19 terrorists who hijacked the commercial airliners on September 11, 2001, provide the most pointed illustration of the radicals' belief. These men carried the promise of Paradise in leader Muhammad Atta's letter of encouragement. The excerpts below offer a chilling look at indoctrination in murder, and at what we must face in the future. Just before the September 11 attack, here is what they read:

Read al-Tawba and Anfal [traditional war chapters from the Quran] and reflect on their meanings and remember all of the things that God has promised for the martyrs. Shouldn't we take advantage of these last hours to offer good deeds and obedience?

This test from Almighty God is to raise your level [of heaven] and erase your sins....Only a few easy seconds separate you from the beginning of a happy life, peaceful life, and the everlasting tranquility with Prophets and the faithful and martyrs. God said: "God will weaken the schemes of the non-believers."

Be happy, optimistic, calm, because you are heading for a deed that God loves and will accept [as a good deed]....Know that the gardens of paradise are waiting for you in all their beauty, and the women of paradise are waiting, calling out, "Come hither, friend of God." They have dressed in their most beautiful clothing.

Open your heart and welcome death for the sake of God. Always, remember to pray if possible before reaching the target or say something like "there is no god but God and Mohamed is His Prophet." After that, God willing, we will meet in Paradise.[140]

Let's be sure about one thing. These terrorists may have, in all sincerity, asked for God's help with their infamous deed—but Paradise is not where they went.

HOW DO TERRORISTS HIJACK ISLAM?

It is important to emphasize again that Muslim radicals do not represent the majority of Muslims. As we have seen however, in certain ways Islam does lend support to the radicals' cause, and this is an important part of the problem. Therefore, in a manner we cannot now predict, the future course of Islam will have a great impact on the future course of the world.

The question is, how did the violent minority emerge on the stage of history in which we now stand? As author Salman Rushdie, under a global death sentence for writing *Satanic*

Verses (about Sura 53:21, which seems to implicate the Prophet in idolatry), suggested, "There needs to be a thorough examination, by Muslims everywhere, of why it is that the faith they love breeds so many violent mutant strains. If the West needs to understand its Unabombers and McVeighs, Islam needs to face up to its Bin Ladens."[141]

Factors for Terrorism

We did not have Muslim terrorists 50 years ago, or just a few at most. Why do we have so many today? Here are some of the most important factors.

- Because of oil reserves and population growth in certain countries, Islam has dramatically increased in power and numbers in the last 50 years.

- The religion of Islam, because of what the Quran teaches, has become the road to world political power for Arabs.

- The birth of Israel in 1948 and its capture of old Jerusalem in 1967 radicalized many Muslims because they believe that the land of Israel belongs to Arabs alone, not to the Jews as the Bible teaches.

- A number of critical events greatly emboldened Arabs and Muslims to seek more power.

    —the Ayatollah Khomeini came to power in Iran, which many Shiite Muslims saw as a fulfillment of an ancient Islamic prophecy that asserted Islam was on the way to world ascendancy. And when Iran humiliated the United States by holding our embassy's personnel hostages, many Muslims came to believe that Islam could attack even America, and America could do nothing about it.

    —The Mujahideen victory over the Soviet Union in Afghanistan was critical in emboldening million of Muslims to believe that Islam actually was superior even to the superpowers.

- Many Muslims saw, especially during the 1990s, the continued expansion of American materialism and an ever-worsening American moral corruption, which further aggravated their disrespect for the U.S.

- Muslims have been further emboldened by U.S. support for the Palestinian cause, and even for a Palestinian state. They see many in America who are very critical of Israel; and they see the U.S. media, in general, supporting Muslim Arab viewpoints and attempting to get the world to "understand" the Muslims' perspective and the Palestinians' many "frustrations."

- Finally, in the eyes of millions of Muslims, Osama bin Laden "brought America to its knees." More than anything else, this is proof to radicals like bin Laden—and their millions of supporters—that Allah is on their side and will destroy America. All this helps explain September 11 and its aftermath.

Arabs and Muslims respect power, not weakness, and the U.S. showed them what they perceived to be weakness. As one Israeli noted of his own nation's situation, "Islam has the concept of acknowledging strength....At present the Jews of Israel appear weak, most of the world is arrayed against us, and the Arabs are smelling blood."[142]

Islam thus has a variety of forces that are working upon it internally and externally. Just as the power of radical Islam has been growing in the last generation, the power of Western influence has made a growing an impact on Islam in its more moderate forms—and it is this influence that has served, in many ways, to radicalize the more fundamental forms of the religion.

Islam's Radicalization

Tens of millions of Muslims worldwide are fundamentalists, many on the fringes of accepting terrorism or something close to it; their presence in the world raises the stakes tremendously. For them, according to one terrorism expert interviewed on CNN, "The United States ranks as the Number One enemy, definitely...."[143] According to another terrorism and security expert, Dr. Jerrold Post of George Washington University, radicalism is now "deeply embedded in Arab society."[144] How has this come to be?

In part, many Muslims have much hatred, much frustration over their own failures—and they need a scapegoat.

For more than 30 years, such Muslim fundamentalists have blamed every setback in the Islamic world—from economic recession to Israeli victories—on what they see as the corruption of classical Islam by Western culture, most of which they see rooted in the United States.[145]

Thus,

In the case of Islam, the many tenets of the Koran that call for mercy, tolerance, patience and charity are simply overridden by those who see their faith in eternal holy war against infidels....The peculiar genius of terrorists like Ayatollah Ruhollah Khomeini or Osama bin Laden has been to persuade their followers that almost all aspects of modern culture...are assaults on Islam for which the only antidote is violence.[146]

For example, though the recent American attacks on Afghanistan were actually very carefully planned operations only against the Taliban and al-Qaeda terrorists, that's not how fundamentalists saw it. Rather, it was an attack on Islam. Religious groups in many Muslim nations responded by calling for a holy war against America, and the "average Muslim in the street" in other places responded with, "This is a holy war, a war between Muslims and Christians."[147]

This is just the attitude that radical terrorists have played on. Islam itself cannot possibly be the source of Muslim problems because Islam came from Allah. And the Quran stresses the world will ultimately be subjected to the will of Allah. Hence, there must be Muslim unity in the face of a "hostile" world that seeks the "annihilation" of Islam. For example, consider the following introductory remarks to M.M. Ali's translation of the Quran. He is summarizing what the Quran teaches about the final victory of Islam, citing specific verses:

The holy Quran claims to be the greatest spiritual force, which is ultimately destined to bring the whole of humanity to perfection....It...will ultimately take hold of the minds of man and before [it] falsehood will vanish....It goes further and lays claim to the fact that it is the only spiritual force which will ultimately conquer the whole world.... All opposition to it is to be swept away....And it is repeated thrice that the Quran was ultimately to prevail over the whole world: "He it is Who has sent His Messenger with the Guidance and the religion of Truth that he may cause it to prevail over all the religions" (61:9; 48:28; 9:33).[148]

...Indeed, we are told that the Quran teaches that all opposition to Islam will be brought to nothing (61: 8).[149]

True Islam?

A good number of Muslims believe that any attempt to associate terrorism with Islam (deserved or not) is part of a global conspiracy to undermine, thwart, or destroy their religion. "We must also recognize that there is a sustained effort to associate Islam and the advocacy of implementing Islam with terrorism. This is part of the worldwide campaign to prevent Islamic revival."[150]

Then we must realize that "one of the Islamic radical movements' greatest successes in the past three decades is their ability to present themselves to a large Muslim public all over the Arab and Muslim world as the bearers of true Islam...."[151] Indeed, a very large number of moderate Muslims aren't too sure that the radicals are *not* the "bearers of true Islam."

In essence, major segments of moderate Islam have been hijacked and terrorized by radical Islam because the radicals have learned to exploit and manipulate many of the frustrations of the moderate Arab–Muslim world, and because significant segments of Islam just aren't sure how to respond. As a result, for example, the September 11 terrorists were not seen as fringe lunatics but were

> widely regarded as heroes within the Arab world. Religious edicts have been issued in Arab countries endorsing the attack, and thousands danced in the streets of the West Bank and Gaza. That pathological response isn't just the result of anger at perceived injustice, but of years of hate indoctrination in mosques and from state-controlled media.[152]

One can but empathize with all the kind and decent Muslims who have had to deal with the aftermath of the atrocities committed by radicals. Many had prayed that the September 11 attackers would not involve their religion, but regrettably, it was not to be—and in fact, terrorism seems to be the new face of much of Islam.

What Can Be Done?

The outcome of the current crisis within Islam cannot be left to chance. Indeed, "The Muslim world today is torn by a deep internal conflict over the essence and purpose of Islamic society. The outcome of this internal conflict has dictated, and continues to dictate, the nature of the ties between Muslim civilization and Western and other Civilizations."[153]

Unless these pro-radical teachings and forces are opposed by others, especially Muslims, then their powers—of persuasion, violence, finance, and propaganda—will grow. If more of Islam is not to be taken hostage by the radical Muslims, moderate Islam must become vastly more engaged in opposing Islamic radicalism. "Islamists, by and large, have come to power when no one is willing to oppose them at home and abroad."[154]

To be sure, Muslim nations that have fought against terrorists in their midst or warned of planned terrorist attacks against the West are to be commended and appreciated. Unfortunately, too many moderate Muslims have tended to look the other way. They have allowed the terrorists to continue their activities unhindered, sometimes even supporting them financially or in other ways, rather than confront the problem on their doorstep. "...The impression is often gained that although radical Islamic Fundamentalism is a minority movement, it appears to have the tacit support of the international Islamic community as such, or at least...a substantial part of that community."[155]

That support will have to change. Moderate Islam knows that the fundamentalists and radicals are Muslims, and they also know that Islam has a serious image problem. For example, Egypt had an "All Islam" conference to tell the world that Islam was not terrorist, because Egyptian Muslims knew that Islamic teaching *was* responsible for the September 11 attacks.

> Humanistic Muslims need to face the lethal consequences of their theology toward non-Muslims. Apologetics about the nobility of Islam aren't good enough anymore....Tolerant Muslims can no longer afford to defend Islam's more problematic concepts.[156]

The Conflict of Muslim Worldviews

Consider the warning of one expert on terrorism (given on September 24, 2001):

> The attacks in the United States have revealed a connection between the fundamentalist ideologies of a number of terrorist groups, all of which profess to act "in the name of Islam." The terrorists who committed suicide in carrying out the attacks in New York and Washington gained legitimacy from a religious ruling by the Egyptian Sheikh Yousef Qaradawi, who ruled that martyrdom was a

"religious commandment and a duty," and that every Muslim should be willing to join the Jihad of martyrdom....His praise of suicide operations to kill Jews and "Crusaders"—Westerners, in other words—helped to plant the seeds of suicide terrorism in America and Europe.

This worldview feeds Islamist extremist movements all over the world, and not just in the Middle East. Groups such as...bin Ladin's al-Qaida, Hizballah, Hamas, and the Palestinian Islamic Jihad all see themselves as engaged in an irreconcilable struggle between cultures, only one of which can survive.

How much of the Islamic world shares these beliefs? It is frequently said that religious figures such as Sheikh Qaradawi represent the more radical fringe of Islam. However, much of the more moderate Islamic mainstream has been quiet and passive in confronting these radicals. If Islamic scholars and leaders of a more peaceful sort do not begin to make themselves heard loudly and clearly, the only voices heard will be the voices of the radicals.[157]

Over a century ago Ernst Renan wrote, "Muslims are the first victims of Islam. I have observed in my travels in the Orient, that fanaticism comes from a small number of dangerous men who maintain the others in the practice of religion by terror." Today it is not only by terror, as with the Taliban of Afghanistan, it is by personal conviction, indoctrination, and promises of a Paradise guaranteed through murderous acts.

This clash of worldviews must be won both by Muslims and by those of influence outside Islam—politicians, intellectuals, and others. Indeed, Western supporters of Islamic radicals need to rethink their loyalties: Are they for civilization and Western values, or for violence and the terrorists? Professor Fred Siegel refers to a Muslim friend and former student who

e-mailed him to say he was "sickened" to watch Middle East-
erners celebrate the terror of September 11. "He wants no
truck with those who kill in the name of Islam." Siegel points
out that it's also fair to ask this conviction of the Western
"rationalizers of Palestinian and Islamic terror." Indeed, "Why
is it that everywhere in the world where Muslims are in the
majority, their minorities are persecuted?"

Professor Siegel wants to know where intellectuals and
European leaders were during the recent U.N. "hate" conference in Durban, South Africa, "when Islamophobia was
denounced, while Muslim discrimination against non-Muslims was passed over in silence...." And as for America, "No
doubt our multiculturalists will explain that, while even mild
anger at Arabs by Americans is a sign of deep-seated racism,
venomous hatred in the Arab world is merely a part of a different culture that can't be judged by our standards."[158] (This,
of course, was the same argument the Nazis gave for their
atrocities during the trials at Nuremburg.)

Muslims' Opportunities

Muslims have great opportunities here. Perhaps the most
important is for the Muslim community in America and
throughout the world to determine very specific ways to effectively deal with the radicals: for instance, by helping other
Muslims understand why radical Islam is evil, by correcting
dangerous misunderstandings, by countering false and treach-
erous propaganda, and by making sure that millions of Muslims around the world understand America is not their enemy.
When it comes to the Quran and Islamic law, a strong apologetic must be sustained that honors Islam's stated commitment
to be a religion of peace, rather than one of pragmatic terror.

In this vein, Rob Sobhani of Georgetown University made
a notable suggestion during a televised interview. He said that
Muslim leaders in America should call a special convention of
the top Islamic leaders in America, however many are necessary. He asserted that it was incumbent upon them to travel to

Muslim fundamentalist leaders around the world, in every nation, with a carefully thought-out plan, and then "get" them to renounce terrorism and to repudiate radicalism. He noted that American special forces and GIs were now sacrificing their lives to defend Americans' freedoms, and would be doing so for years. They would be sacrificing their lives to protect all Americans—Muslims included—from more terrorist attacks. Muslims therefore, he said, were obligated to America for at least that much.[159]

Muslim Americans have benefited greatly from our freedoms and our prosperity—even some of the terrorists who want to destroy the U.S. concede as much. So, we agree that American Muslim leaders have a debt to repay for September 11. Indeed, if the radicals gain too much influence, America may have problems with its own 2 million believers, not to mention what Europe will face with its 60 million Muslims.

WHAT IS THE RELATIONSHIP OF AMERICAN MUSLIMS TO RADICAL ISLAM?

American Muslims consist of a majority of moderates with a minority of radicals who, though they were subdued after the September 11 massacre, remained committed to radicalizing U.S. Muslims nonetheless. Muslim scholars and clerics in America, hopefully, are taking steps to more strongly support moderate sentiments and thoroughly condemn all radical convictions, including what undergirds and supports them.

On September 11, the American Muslim Political Coordination Council (AMPCC) released a statement that read in part,

> American Muslims utterly condemn what are apparently vicious and cowardly acts of terrorism against innocent civilians....[160]

The statement also offered condolences to the families of those who were killed or injured.

But other reactions among U.S. Muslims, especially the powerful Islamic lobby, illustrate that the American Muslim community has work to do. "We do not judge Islam by what a few Muslims do. We judge Islam by what is said in the Quran."[161] "Americans, don't let this tragedy be in vain. Wake up and realise that you cannot ignore the injustices your government commits abroad. The American government is hated for many reasons— it is time to consider these and make changes."[162]

At the Islam.org Web site, here is how American Muslims voted recently on a variety of issues. (The poll was unscientific and voluntary, hence not authoritative; all but one question was asked before September 11.)

- Responding to the question, "Do you agree with the tactic of so-called suicide bombing in Palestine?" an incredible 46 percent agreed with suicide bombings.

- In response to the query: "In the wake of the terrorist bombings in the U.S. and the subsequent anti-Muslim backlash,…what is the most important thing Muslims should focus on?" 56 percent said, "Provide assistance to the victims"; 27 percent answered, "Actively defend Muslim Rights."

- Fully 94 percent said "yes" in response to this question about Israel's prime minister: "Should Ariel Sharon be tried for crimes against humanity?"[163]

Influences on American Muslims

Some of the above responses seem to indicate that America may encounter a problem with radical Muslims within its own borders if Islamic clerics do not more forcefully teach that their religion is peaceful and utterly repudiate violence. One American Muslim commentator remarks,

> When enlightened imams lead mosques and inspire
> their congregations to actively promote what is right
> and oppose what is wrong, the risks of some deviants
> pulling off malevolent deeds are either minimized or
> made easier to identify and thwart. Only then will
> America and the world begin to appreciate the true,
> peaceful message of Islam.[164]

On the other hand, there is good reason to take a less hopeful view. For example, Sheikh Kabbani of the Islamic Supreme Council declared at the U.S. State Department in January 1999 that extremist views—not terrorist views, but those that may lead to terrorist views—have taken over "80 percent of the mosques in the United States." (How this specifically relates to attendees' beliefs is undetermined.)[165] In addition, the Muslim Brethren (founded in Egypt in 1929 and a major global exporter of radical Wahhabi teachings) are said to have "sister" organizations in the U.S. These include the powerful, radical Council on Islamic Relations (CAIR) in Washington, D.C., which actively seeks to silence criticism of Islam it deems offensive; and the American Muslim Council (AMC), which is said to train almost all Muslim chaplains for the U.S. Army![166] One Muslim source stated that "the great majority of all mosques in Democratic countries—not only in North America, but in most of Western Europe as well—are controlled by extremists."[167]

We don't know whether these claims are true, but obviously, determining the degree of extremism in Western mosques and effectively countering it should become a priority for democracies. In newspaper and other articles, Dr. Daniel Pipes and others have thoroughly uncovered the agenda of Islam's radical lobby in America and the West, and it is not appealing.[168] For example,

> The terror attacks on America could not have
> taken place without a sophisticated infrastructure
> of agents operating inside the United State that

gathered information, planned, and then executed the four hijackings. That infrastructure, in turn, could operate thanks in large part to the protection provided by America's militant Islamic lobby."[169]

Moreover, others have issued warnings about Muslim views of America abroad that tend to influence Muslims here.

What does the future for Islam in America hold? One thing I am certain of; it holds terrorism. I've studied Islamic viewpoints on America. The majority of Muslims today view America as the last great wall that stops Islam. In their mind, America must be destroyed or brought down, by any means necessary. This is what motivated Sheik Rahman to blow up the New York towers. This is what motivates Muslims throughout America to speak of a day when America will fall to Islam's power.[170]

Terrorist leaders are often intellectuals and have lived in America and the West, attended their graduate schools, studied their cultures, learned their languages. Many radicals actually "like" America and consider themselves to be acting in America's best interests—by employing terror to help institute *sharia* (Islamic law). Eyad Ismail, one of the World Trade Center bombers (in 1993), "Loved everything American from cowboy movies to hamburgers," according to his brother. His sister "recalled his love of U.S. television and his saying, 'I want to live in America forever.'" The family, she commented, "always considered him a son of America." In a statement that sums up this whole outlook, an Islamist in Washington asserted, "I listen to Mozart; I read Shakespeare; I watch the Comedy Channel; and I also believe in the implementation of the Shari'a [Islamic sacred law]."[171]

The Future Outlook

In spite of what has been said, Americans should understand that Islam clearly does have positive teachings about God, man, and relationships among men. It is these that American Muslims must emphasize. Consider the following verses in the Quran:

> Allah does not forbid you to be kind and to act equitably toward those who have not fought you because of your religion...Allah loves those who are equitable (Sura 60:8-9).

> ...But forgive them, and overlook (their misdeeds): for Allah loveth those who are kind...(5:13).

> O mankind, surely we have created you from a male and a female, and made you tribes and families that you may know each other (49:13).

> But if the enemy incline towards peace, do thou (also) incline towards peace, and trust in Allah (8:61).

One wonders what America would look like should Muslims of various persuasions come to power in the U.S. overnight. How would they see and implement the mission of Islam?

It is the above scriptures that, we hope, will have dominance in the Islam of the future, and especially in America, where American Muslims will have the opportunity to convince their brethren around the world that America is not the enemy many think it is. They live here, they know—one hopes. Even after the brutal September 11 attack by the terrorists, the vast majority of Americans showed Muslims incredible graciousness. There were only a relatively small number of incidents of verbal or physical attacks against Muslims or their property. Too many, yes—but not proof that America is the archenemy of all Islam.

Is Radical Muslim Terrorism Non-Islamic?

We have touched on this subject briefly in other chapters and have suggested that the answer to this question is "no." In the next two chapters we wish to explain the reasons we feel this way.

Radical Islam is referred to in various terms—the Islamic Resurgence, Islamic militancy, radical Islamic fundamentalism, Islamism, or perhaps more appropriately, the global *jihad* movement. Some have called it a struggle for the "heart and soul of Islam."

Whether radical Muslim terrorism is Islamic depends on your view of Islam. Certainly, radical Islam is not how the religion is practiced by the majority of Muslims, who are nonviolent. Much of Islamic history and interpretation of the *sharia* also opposes the radicals. But their message would not find the success it has had were there not *some* supporting basis within Islam. Three "supports" for their message are *Kharijism, Wahhabism,* and *jihad.*

Two Forms of Islam

Kharijism was an early sect in Islam that fits quite well with modern radical Islam. In early Islam, a civil war was fought over the "true" successor to Muhammad, a conflict that led to the division between the majority Sunni and minority Shiite branches of Islam. A group later named the Kharajites ("withdrawers") believed that only God could determine the proper successor, and that He would let His will be known in battle.

The Kharajites

> held that any person who strayed from the perfect practice of Islam was ipso facto an apostate and could be killed. And they believed that only they

had the true notion of what Islam required. They applied their doctrine with a ferocity against both the developing Sunni and Shi'a traditions of Islam....Their tactics were frightfully violent, and it took centuries before they were put down.[172]

Kharijism's uncompromising nature produced several sub-sects, both moderate and extreme. Particular doctrines common to all Kharijite sects include the idea that a believer who commits a mortal sin is an apostate, and that all non-Kharijites are infidels.[173] "Kharijite uprisings continued...in Iraq, Iran, and Arabia;...Kharijism was suppressed in Iraq but continued to play an important political role in eastern Arabia, North Africa, and eastern Africa. Kharijism survives today in these areas."[174]

The form of Islam called *Wahhabism* also lends itself to extremists like bin Laden. *Muwahhidun,* the term used by followers, was founded by Muhammad ibn 'Abd al-Wahhab (1703–1792) in Saudi Arabia, and is predicated on the Sunni teachings of Ibn Hanbal (780–855). Al-Wahhab taught that all additions to Islam after the third century of the Muslim era (after about 950) were unauthentic and must be erased. *Muwahhidun* became an inspiration to other Islamic reform movements from India and Sumatra to North Africa and the Sudan. (The Afghani Taliban might be considered its cousin.)

The theology and law of *Muwahhidun* emphasize a literal belief in the Quran and Hadith (sayings attributed to Muhammad), and the establishment of a Muslim state based entirely on Islamic law. (In this view, as we have noted before, God does not distinguish between human races, nations, or tribes, but perceives only one division in the entire human race: that between believer and nonbeliever.) Wahhabism's ultimate purpose is to bring about a global revolution based on Wahhabi teachings, which is probably why believers in Saudi Arabia have exported it far and wide.

A Restoration?

Because of these traditions in Islam, as well as other factors, radicals such as Osama bin Laden believe they are restoring "true" Islam. "Bin Laden and other Islamic radicals claim they represent ancient Islam. It is true that they do represent one tradition in Islam, but it is a tradition that Islam early on rejected as opposed to the universal message of its Prophet."[175] Nonetheless, the radicals believe that by returning to the historic roots of Arab and Muslim greatness—a greatness to be restored by the unification of all Arab states under "pure" Islam—Islam will rise to its true destiny.

Because much other Islamic tradition also divides the world into two opposing camps, the *dar al-Islam* (the realm of Islam) and the *dar al-harb* (the realm of war), between which there is to be unending conflict, the radicals feel further justified in their point of view, and believe that Islam is destined for victory by Allah.

So, these things are what radicals have seized on, and unfortunately, as we know, they are persuading moderates. Many moderates do think in these terms to varying degrees, though their interpretations may be softer—for example, the "war" is personal and internal, and it is possible to have a successful "land of Islam" in a country even though Muslims remain in minority. But in spite of what moderates may believe, and even though the radicals do not completely represent true Islam today, they do have a basis in Islamic history for their beliefs.

DOES ISLAM TEACH A DOCTRINE OF *JIHAD*, AND WHAT RELATIONSHIP DOES THIS HAVE TO TERRORISM?

> Fighting is prescribed upon you, and you dislike it. But it may happen that you dislike a thing which is good for you, and it may happen that you love a

thing which is bad for you. And Allah knows and
you know not (Sura 2:216).

Muslims are divided over the issue of *jihad*. In brief, we can
say that while the Quran does teach *jihad* (for example, Suras
4:74,76; 8:12,39-42; 8:15,16; 9:39), as far as its military aspect
is concerned, Muslims disagree about both its relevance and
meaning for today. All Muslims do accept the concept. The
term itself means "struggle," and there are many different
forms of struggle that may be engaged in by a Muslim—spiritual, psychological, social, and physical; or even intellectual,
that is, the struggle of intellectual warfare against one's perceived enemies in order to protect or expand the faith: "So
obey not the rejecters of faith, but strive *[jahidhum]* against
them by it [the Quran] with a great endeavor" (25:52).

Military Conflict in the Quran

The soft side of the term appears to be emphasized in
moderate Islam, but clearly, the military concept of a "holy
war" campaign is increasing in popularity in many places.
The term *jihad* in this sense has been invoked throughout
the Islamic world by fundamentalists in order to "protect"
Islam. The Taliban in Afghanistan, the al-Qaeda terrorist
group, and Muslims in Pakistan, Palestine, the Sudan,
Kashmir, and other places where there are Muslim conflicts
have all called upon Muslims to engage in a "holy war" to
"defend" their religion.

Though terrorism is forbidden in most Islam, the difficulty
is that those who advocate it do so by appealing to a literal
interpretation of the Quran.

> According to Khaled Abou El Fadl, an acting pro-
> fessor at UCLA law school, Islamic law considers
> terrorism (hirabah) a grave and predatory sin pun-
> ishable by death. It forbids the taking or slaying of
> hostages as well as stealthy or indiscriminate

attacks against enemies....But, he argues that an "ethically oblivious" strand of Islam has developed since the 1970s that dismisses the juristic tradition and the notion of universal and innate moral values. Instead, it relies on a literal interpretation of texts and the technicalities of Islamic law...."[176]

The radicals see *jihad* and terrorism in the Quran, and that is all that matters to them. Allah, through believers, "shall cast terror into the hearts of the infidels" (for example, Sura 5:33; 8:12-14). The way in which *jihad* relates to terrorism is that *jihad,* for the Muslim radicals, *is* terrorism. As we saw with bin Laden, *jihad* is the terrorist war waged on the apostate Muslims, the infidel, and the American and Western "aggressors" against Islam. In declaring *jihad,* bin Laden and his fellow radicals are convinced that they are interpreting the Quran accurately—and that they are responding appropriately to aggression against Islam allegedly initiated by the West, in particular America.

While the term "holy war" per se is not found in the Quran, the doctrine of military conflict against one's enemies is very clearly taught.

The word *jihad* comes from the Arabic word *jahada,* which, as Lane in his celebrated *Arabic-English Lexicon* points out, means "He strove, laboured, or toiled; exerted himself or his power or efforts or endeavours or ability." *Jihad,* continues Lane, "properly signifies using or exerting, one's utmost power, efforts, endeavours, or ability, in contending with an object of disapprobation, and this of three kinds, namely, a visible enemy, the devil, and one's self; all of which are included in the Quran sura xxii.78....*Jihad* came to be used by the Muslim to signify generally 'he fought, warred, or waged war,' against unbelievers and the like."[177]

"Defensive" War

The military concept of *jihad* is usually (not always) defensive in the Quran—defending oneself against unsought hostilities or aggression. The problem is that in practice, "defensive" *jihad* can be interpreted conceptually to incorporate offensive military action when Islam seems threatened, or apparently even when Islam seeks to "liberate" "oppressed" peoples. In history, holy wars have been fought both defensively and offensively. "Defending Islam" can mean different things to different Muslims, depending on varying circumstances and personal interests.

Consider Sura 61:9, which is cited in the Hadith as a *jihad* verse. "He it is who has sent His Messenger with the guidance and the true religion that he may make it overcome all (other) religions."[178] Here is another translation: "He it is Who sent His messenger with the guidance and the true religion, that He may make it overcome the religions, all of them."[179]

The translator of the latter version ties this verse to the two previous verses, which he considers prophecies:

> ...It is affirmed that Islam will be made the predominant religion, the truth of which was witnessed by Arabia in the lifetime of the Holy Prophet. But both prophecies have a wider significance. Attempts are still being made to *annihilate Islam,* and the Divine promise is that all these attempts shall be brought to naught; while the predominance of Islam over all the religions of the world would in time be established, as clearly as it was in Arabia.[180]

Islam will finally conquer all religions and the world of unbelief, and if they are not willing to be conquered voluntarily, one might see how some Muslims would seek to fulfill the "Divine promise" by involuntary means.

Interpreting "Annihilation"

Seeking to "annihilate Islam" can, some argue, be something as innocent as criticizing the prophet, Islam, or the Quran. Christians who share their faith in Jesus are, in their own way, seeking to "annihilate" Islam, because many Muslims are taken from the faith.

Thus, referring to those who are said to "forge a lie against Allah," the same translator mentioned above refers to the transgressors as either polytheists, or "the Christians are meant who were invited to the Truth, but they forged a lie that Jesus was the son of God and that he took away their sins."[181]

In essence, *jihad*, military or otherwise, can be exercised offensively or defensively and that "protecting Islam from annihilation" may involve warring against even *ideas* that oppose Islam.

Consider the following statement of Muhammad in the Hadith:

> I have been commanded that I should fight these people till they bear witness that there is no God but Allah and keep up prayer and pay zakat [taxes]. When they do this, their blood and their property shall be safe with me except as Islam requires....[182]

The commentary on this verse first points out that

> the command to fight is contained in the holy Quran....Muslims, therefore, could not resort to fighting unless the enemy was the first to assume hostilities....What the hadith means is that fighting begun under these conditions is to cease when the enemy people accept Islam.[183]

Muslim radicals like bin Laden, many fundamentalists, and even some moderate Muslims all believe that America, by its defense of Kuwait and "aggression" against Iraq in the Gulf

War, and by its "aggression" against Afghanistan's Taliban and the al-Qaeda organization, did indeed become "the first to assume hostilities."

Some Muslim scholars argue that the Quranic passages with unconditional declarations of *jihad* must be interpreted in light of the conditional passages that speak principally of defensive *jihad*. But even when trying to support defensive *jihad*, they seem to find it difficult to defend a "conditional" interpretation, not only because other Islamic scholars disagree with them, but because they concede that, given the right conditions, *jihad* can become an offensive measure to protect Islam from its enemies.[184]

We have already seen that Christians may be interpreted as those who are attempting to "annihilate Islam." Is it possible that *jihad* against them may be rationalized, as is currently the case in the inhuman war on Christians in the Sudan? Radicals argue that, merely by their teachings about Jesus Christ, Christians have already committed the worst of sins against Islam and have begun hostilities, seeking to take Muslims away from the Islamic faith. By designating Jesus as God, Christians have blasphemed Allah and committed an unforgivable sin, termed *shirk*. For radicals, the hostilities will end only when the "aggressors" or "enemy peoples" accept Islam.

What Kind of Future?

Radical Islamic fundamentalism has a very specific vision for the future. As Iranian Muslim Ayatullah Morteza Mutahhari wrote in *The Holy War of Islam and Its Legitimacy in the Quran*, "Islam came to reform society and to form a nation and government. Its mandate is the reform of the whole world. Such a religion cannot be indifferent. It cannot be without a law of jihad."[185]

Most importantly, in this war to "reform the whole world" *jihad* can be offensive, not defensive. The "defense" of Islam is interpreted as including offensive measures:

> So, when we say that the basis of jihad is defense, we do not mean defense in the limited sense of having to defend oneself when one is attacked with the sword, gun or artillery shell. No, we mean that [Islamically speaking] if one's being, one's material or spiritual values are aggressed or in fact, if something that mankind values and respects and which is necessary for mankind's prosperity and happiness [for example, Islam], is aggressed, then we are to defend it....The meaning of defense is so wide that it includes the defense of spiritual values.... However, [the idea of "no compulsion in religion"] does not...mean that, if we see..."No God but Allah" being threatened from some direction, we are not to defend it. No, not at all.[186]

Some Muslims will disagree with this, but that's the point—other Muslims disagree with *them*. Once again, this is all the Muslim radicals are doing in their terrorism against America—simply exercising their right to "defend Islam" by engaging in an offensive *jihad* interpreted defensively. (Bin Laden expressed it perfectly—no innocents, not even little children.)

A final point is that Muhammad simply would not have succeeded in conquering Arabia had he preached only peace, humility, and submission.

> Muslim theologians are unanimous in declaring that no religious toleration was extended to the idolaters of Arabia at the time of Muhammad. The only choice given them was death or the acceptance of Islam. This total intolerance never seems to be taken into consideration by the apologists of Islam when they lay claims to Islamic tolerance.[187]

If, as some argue, the future of Islam is based on the future of its interpretation of *jihad,* then the world needs to pay particular attention to precisely how the global Islamic community views "holy war."

What Else About Radical Islam Should Concern Us?

As vital as the war on terrorism is, there is something yet more important. The world now faces the possibility that Islam will become increasingly radicalized—that fundamentalists will seek ever more actively to depose moderate governments and attempt to form a united "Islamic Empire" or bloc of nations that will oppose America and the democratic West as the epitome of anti-Islamic influence in the world.

We hope, of course, that the war on terrorism will drastically stunt the growth of radical Islam—but only time will tell. It's the "average" Muslim in the world who is "on the chessboard," and we do not know how this perilous game will be played out.

We should note the extent to which American and Western leaders had to "walk softly" in their response to the attacks on the U.S. so as to not offend global Islam. Initial policies and military plans were scuttled or revised out of concern for radicalizing more Muslims around the world, and other policies were also changed. Clearly then, Islam and the forces at work within it pose a potential future danger, one so serious that even now America and the West can't always act the way they think they should act, even after an attack like that of September 11.

In 1998, one of the nation's foremost authorities on Muslim nationalism, Anthony Dennis, pointed out that for years, Muslim radicals and terrorists have been "actively working toward either political unification or some form of the Islamic Confederation...." Further, the radicals are winning the battle for the hearts of the moderate Muslim populace:

...As far as the contest between Islam versus democracy, I think political Islam is winning hands down in the contest for the "hearts and minds" of the people in the Muslim world. The fundamentalists speak a political language and articulate a vision for a religious dictatorship that harkens back to early Muslim history and is a vision for the future that many traditional Muslims can understand. These groups know this too....They consciously attempt to work across borders with one another to coordinate their efforts. They are actively working toward either political unification or some form of Islamic Confederation, as I call it. This is the great unreported story in the Western media, indeed in any media.[188]

A Dangerous Prospect

If fundamentalist dictatorships are installed in key "moderate" Muslim nations like Egypt, or in Turkey, then we will face an extremely dangerous situation in which democracy has almost no chance throughout the Muslim world. Says Dennis,

> I believe that the fundamentalist movement will eventually pose a hemispheric and ultimately a global military threat for several reasons. First, their avowed hostility and hatred of all things Western makes the U.S. and indeed Western culture and civilization a natural enemy of theirs. Second, they are on their way to becoming a global threat because as they rise to power in additional countries their military capabilities and strength will accordingly increase....[With weapons of mass destruction,] they may finally have found a way to strike back at "the Great Satan," as they call us, with more than just simple acts of terrorism.[189]

As Dennis points out, the problem currently is not Islam, but Islamic radicalism. Nevertheless, Islam as a religion will have to decide what it will do with the specific causes of highly dangerous fundamentalism within its ranks—causes supported by the Quran, by precedents of religiously justified *jihad* in Islamic history, by Islamic law *(sharia)* and tradition, and by other features of Islam.

33

WHAT OPPORTUNITY DOES THE CONFLICT WITH ISLAMIC TERRORISM PRESENT TO CHRISTIANS?

Millions of people today no longer feel secure about much of anything, and they are more open than ever to discussing the big questions about life. In fact, millions of Americans are just plain scared. So for Christians the doors are, and should remain, wide open to share their faith—to show people why Christianity is objectively true, that God loves them, is sovereign and in control—and to explain how a personal relationship with Jesus Christ can answer their deepest concerns and needs, now and forever. This applies especially to Muslims. On September 11, it became much more difficult for Muslims to live in America. Christians can show heartfelt acts of compassion, understanding, and assistance that will reflect the love of Jesus Christ for Muslims and for others.

Perhaps by stressing common cultural concerns, Christians and Muslims may find a door opened to a frank discussion of their differing religious beliefs. Muslims in the West, much like Christians, are often frustrated with the culture in which they live. Given the Western worldview of materialism, secularism, and relativism, and its moral failings as seen in the crime and divorce rates, mass abortion, pornography, and other ills, both Muslims and Christians can find common ground on which to discuss the larger issues of their religions.

Christians can take this opportunity—which will exist for the foreseeable future—to help Muslims understand that they respect and care for them as individuals *because of* their distinctively Christian beliefs. Muslims and Christians can frankly examine what their faiths teach about the crucial issues of the nature of God, salvation, Scripture, and Jesus Christ, and the evidential bases upon which both faiths place their convictions. (At the end of this book we have supplied a brief resource list of useful information.)

Most importantly, Christians need to recognize the power of the gospel of Jesus Christ and the Word of God in any discussion of religious beliefs. Muslims have great faith in Allah and Muhammad and the Quran, but they also have no assurance of salvation within the confines of their own religion. And they desperately yearn for this. Christians can help Muslims to understand that salvation is a free gift based on God's grace because of what Jesus Christ accomplished on the cross, "for God so loved the world, that He gave His only begotten Son that whosoever believes in Him shall not perish, but have eternal life" (Jn. 3:16).

A Personal Word—
What Can Muslims Do Who Desire to Know That They Have Eternal Life?

If you are a Muslim who is willing to accept the evidence and who desires to *know* that you have eternal life, what can you do? Jesus promises that all who believe on Him can know, at this moment, that they possess eternal life.

> This is eternal life, that they may *know* You, the only true God, and Jesus Christ whom You have sent (Jn. 17:3).

> Truly, truly, I say uto you, he who believes *has eternal life* (Jn. 6:47).

> I tell you the truth, whoever hears my word and believes him who sent me *has eternal life* and will not be condemned; he has *crossed over* from death to life (Jn. 5:24).

> My sheep listen to my voice; I know them, and they follow me. *I give them eternal life,* and they shall *never perish;* no one can snatch them out of my hand (Jn. 10:27-28).

If you have longed for a personal relationship with God, a relationship in which you *know* that God loves you, and yet have been unable to find this, then the true God offers you this opportunity. God tells us that "all have sinned and fall short of the glory of God" (Rom. 3:23). But God has promised us full forgiveness of sins (Heb. 10:14) if we turn from our sin and turn to Christ, believing on Him for salvation: "The wages of sin is death, but the gift of God is eternal life in Christ Jesus our Lord" (Rom. 6:23).

> God so loved the world that he gave his one and only Son, that whoever believes in him shall not perish but have eternal life. For God did not send his Son into the world to condemn the world, but to save the world through him. Whoever believes in him is not condemned, but whoever does not believe stands condemned already because he has not believed in the name of God's one and only Son (Jn. 3:16-18).

And,

> We accept man's testimony, but God's testimony is greater because it is the testimony of God, which he has given about his Son. Anyone who

believes in the Son of God has this testimony in his heart. Anyone who does not believe God has made him out to be a liar, because he has not believed the testimony God has given about his Son. And this is the testimony: God has given us eternal life, and this life is in his Son. He who has the Son has life; he who does not have the Son of God does not have life. I write these things to you who believe in the name of the Son of God so that you may know that you have eternal life (1 Jn. 5:9-13).

If you sincerely desire to know God personally, you can know that your sins are forgiven and that a place in heaven is reserved for you (1 Pet. 1:4-5) by praying the following prayer to receive Jesus Christ as your personal Lord and Savior:

> *Dear God,*
>
> *I acknowledge my sinfulness before You. I confess that I have been trying to earn my own salvation. But I now see my need for forgiveness in Christ, who died for my sins on the cross. I now receive Him as my personal Savior and Lord. Give me courage and strength to face the opposition I may encounter. Help me to lead others to You as well. In Jesus' name I pray. Amen.*

If you have prayed this prayer, please write us at *The John Ankerberg Show* so we may send you some helpful materials about growing in the Christian life. (Our address is P.O. Box 8977, Chattanooga, TN 37414-0977.)

We also recommend that you begin to read the New Testament to know more about the true Jesus Christ. In addition, attend a church that honors Christ as Lord and the Bible as God's Word. Talk to God daily in prayer.

The following books will help you grow in the Christian life:

- J.I. Packer, *God's Words* (InterVarsity)
- Francis Schaeffer, *True Spirituality* (Tyndale)
- Abdiyah Akbar Abdul-Haqq, *Sharing Your Faith with a Muslim* (Bethany)
- William Miller, *Ten Muslims Meet Christ* (Eerdmans)
- Mark Hannah, *The True Path: Seven Muslims Make Their Greatest Discovery* (International Doorways)

ON JIHAD

If one reads encyclopedias, dictionaries, texts on Islam, commentators, the Hadith, and the Quran, it becomes clear that *jihad* can be both offensive and defensive; it just depends on the interpretation. In illustration, here are some excerpts from the Quran that seem to allow the widest kind of interpretation (even a terroristic interpretation); they are followed by Muslim writers and scholars' comments on the concept of *jihad*.

> God will bring to nothing the deeds of those who disbelieve and debar others from His path....The unbelievers follow falsehood, while the faithful follow truth....When you meet the unbelievers in the battlefield strike off their heads and, when you have laid them low, bind your captives firmly. Then grant them their freedom or take a ransom from them, until War shall lay down her burdens. Thus shall you do. Had God willed, He could Himself have punished them; [but He has ordained it thus] that he may test you, the one by the other. As for those who are slain in the cause of God, He will not

allow their works to perish. He will vouchsafe them guidance and ennoble their state; He will admit them to the Paradise He has made known to them (47:1:,3,5).

Against them make ready your strength to the utmost of your power, including steeds of war, to strike terror into (the hearts of) the enemies, of Allah and your enemies, and others besides, whom ye may not know, but whom Allah doth know. Whatever ye shall spend in the cause of Allah, shall be repaid unto you, and ye shall not be treated unjustly (8:60).

Soon shall We cast terror into the hearts of the Unbelievers, for that they joined companions with Allah, for which He had sent no authority: their abode will be the Fire: And evil is the home of the wrong-doers! (3:15).

…They press their fingers in their ears to keep out the stunning thunder-clap, the while they are in terror of death. But Allah is ever round the rejecters of Faith! (2:19).

Remember thy Lord inspired the angels (with the message): "I am with you: give firmness to the Believers: I will instill terror into the hearts of the Unbelievers: smite ye above their necks and smite all their finger-tips off them" (8:12).

Allah sets forth a Parable: a city enjoying security and quiet, abundantly supplied with sustenance from every place: Yet was it ungrateful for the favours of Allah. So Allah made it taste of hunger and terror (in extremes) (closing in on it) like a garment (from every side) because of the (evil) which (its people) wrought (16:112).

And those of the People of the Book [Christians and Jews] who aided them—Allah did take them down from their strongholds and cast terror into their hearts. (So that) some ye slew, and some ye made prisoners (33:26).

.... And they thought that their fortresses would defend them from Allah. But the (Wrath of) Allah came to them from quarters from which they little expected (it), and cast terror into their hearts... (59:2).

• • •

Definition of Jihad: not an attempt to convert people to Islam by force (except maybe in the 1st century of Islam). Rather, attempt to "expand and extend Islam until the whole world is under Muslim rule. The jihad is essentially a permanent state of hostility that Islam maintains against the rest of the world, with or without fighting for more sovereignty over more territory." It is a duty, an obligation for all Muslims.[190]

Jihad can be both defence, as well as attacking an enemy.[191]

Muslims had to fight their battles, but this they had to do simply to defend the Islam which unbelievers wanted to annihilate....Muslims were told to be always ready, if the need arose, to defend the Faith with the sword, that being the way to Paradise.[192]

The mission of the Prophet Muhammad...was to free people from tyranny and exploitation by oppressive systems....After...the conquest of Syria and Iraq by the Muslims, the Christian population of Hims reportedly said to the Muslims: "We like your rule and justice far better than the state of oppression and tyranny under which we have been living...."[193]

All acts of war are permitted in the Dar ul Harb ["land of unbelievers"].[194]

Nor are even the People of the Book (principally Christians and Jews) necessarily safe.

> This is the view of some of the Quranic commentators. To them, when the Quran tells us we are to fight against the People of the Book, it means that we are to fight against all the People of the Book, that the faith in God of not one of them is a valid faith; that the faith in the resurrection and in what God has forbidden and permitted of not one of them is valid....A different group of commentators, however,...[argues] it is not with all the People of the Book that we are to fight, but a group from amongst them.[195]

> Since lawful warfare is essentially jihad and since its aim is that the religion is God's entirely [2:189; 8:39] and God's word is uppermost [9:40], therefore, according to all Muslims, those who stand in the way of this aim must be fought. As for those who cannot offer resistance or cannot fight, such as women, children, monks, old people, the blind, handicapped and their likes, they shall not be killed, unless they actually fight with words (e.g. by propaganda) and acts (e.g. by spying or otherwise assisting in the warfare). Some (jurists) are of the opinion that all of them may be killed, on the mere ground that they are unbelievers, but they make an exception for women and children since they constitute property for Muslims. However, the first opinion is the correct one, because we may only fight those who fight us when we want to make God's religion victorious.[196]

> "The word jihad means fighting only, fighting with the sword."[197]

As Tyan in his article in the EI (Djihad, I.538 ff.) makes clear, "in law, according to general doctrine and in historical tradition, the jihad consists of military action with the object of the expansion of Islam and, if need be, of its defence." Tyan expressly rules out the thesis of a wholly apologetic character, according to which Islam relies on peaceful expansion, and that jihad is only authorized in cases of self-defence. This thesis ignores entirely the doctrines developed by Muslim theologians, the historical tradition, as well as texts of the Quran and sunna. Another scholar, Rudolph Peters...also emphasizes that Classical Muslim Quran interpretation regarded the Sword Verses of the Quran... with unconditional command to fight the unbelievers, as having abrogated all previous verses concerning relations with non-Muslims.[198]

"Hadith after hadith recounts in horrible details as to how the jihad against infidels was to be carried out;...they do not talk of metaphorical battles, or allegorical, spiritual struggles, but bloody war." Many samples are cited from Bukhari, Muslim and other traditionists. Bukhari: "Verily Allah has purchased of the believers their lives and their properties; for theirs (in return) is Paradise. They fight in His cause, so they kill (others) and are killed."... Samurah B. Jundub reported the Apostle of Allah (may peace be upon him) as saying: "Kill the old men who are polytheists, but spare their children." Averroes: "Scholars agree that jihad is collective not a personal obligation....According to the majority of scholars, the compulsory nature of the jihad is founded on sura 2:216 'Prescribed for you is fighting, though it be hateful to you.'... Scholars agree that all polytheists should be fought. This is founded on sura 8:39 'Fight them until there is no persecution and the religion is God's entirely.'" Ibn Khaldun: "In the Muslim community, the holy war is a religious duty, because of the universalism of the Muslim mission and the obligation to convert everybody either by persuasion or by force."[199]

Ibn Warraq:
Is Islam Itself Moderate?

In his book *Why I Am Not a Muslim*, former Muslim Ibn Warraq describes the book as "an uncompromising and critical look at almost all the fundamental tenets of Islam." The book itself was motivated by the notorious Salman Rushdie affair and the Muslim-instituted war in the Sudan, Iran, Saudi Arabia, and Pakistan—"war whose principal victims are Muslims, Muslim women, Muslim intellectuals, writers, ordinary decent people." Says the author, "This book is my war effort. Each time I have doubted the wisdom of writing such a book, new murders in the name of God and Islam committed in Algeria or Iran or Turkey or the Sudan have urged me on to complete it."[200] He later goes on to say,

> Sayyid Qutb, the very influential Egyptian Muslim thinker, said that "dominion should be reverted to Allah alone, namely to Islam, that holistic system He conferred upon men. An all-out offensive, a jihad, should be waged against modernity so that this moral rearmament could take place. The ultimate objective is to re-establish the Kingdom of Allah upon earth...."[201]

Of Islamic fundamentalism, Warraq notes,

> There may be moderate Muslims, but Islam itself is
> not moderate. There is no difference between Islam
> and Islamic fundamentalism: at most there is a dif-
> ference of degree but not of kind. All the tenets of
> Islamic fundamentalism are derived from the
> Quran, the Sunna, and the Hadith—Islamic fun-
> damentalism is a totalitarian construct derived by
> Muslim jurists from the fundamental and defining
> texts of Islam. The fundamentalists, with greater
> logic and coherence than so-called moderate or lib-
> eral Muslims, have made Islam the basis of a rad-
> ical utopian ideology that aims to replace
> capitalism and democracy as the reigning world
> system…. Islamic fundamentalism has global aspi-
> rations: the submission of the entire world to the
> all-embracing Shari'a, Islamic Law, a fascist system
> of dictates designed to control every single act of all
> individuals.[202]

He points out the Westerners in general and Americans in
particular simply have no understanding of the true nature of
the Islamic terrorists and what motivates them, observing that
jihad is "an incumbent religious duty, established in the Quran
and the Traditions as a divine institution" with the purpose of
advancing Islam and repelling evil from Muslims.[203]

APPENDIX C

WHO ARE THE TERRORISTS?

Merely a generation ago, it would have been difficult to find more than a score of well-organized terrorist groups in the world. Today, although it is impossible to know the exact number of groups, it is certainly in the hundreds, with hundreds of thousands of members. SpecialOperations.com lists about 600 terrorist groups around the globe. Other sources say there are about 280 active terrorist groups in the world. Though overall membership cannot be determined, 30 of these groups allegedly account for 200,000 to 300,000 active members. (The Terrorism Research Center [Terrorism.com] lists about 100 terrorist groups, offering profiles on each. This Web site provides much useful information on the subject.)[204]

Many terrorist groups actively employ front organizations, such as businesses and charities, and seek to gain legitimacy in the eyes of the public. (Witness the PLO, which has become the "darling" terror organization of so many in Europe and the West.)

Terrorism has become a global concern, and is now considered the single most serious national security threat to the United States.

As we saw earlier in this book, radical Islam—perhaps Islam itself—provides fertile ground for the breeding of terrorist beliefs. Even as we write, militant Islamic groups officially described as international terrorist organizations—Hezbollah, HAMAS, Palestine Islamic Jihad, and many others—are operating quietly within the borders of the United States. Many are on the run, but are also regrouping and restrategizing. (HAMAS militants' surveillance operations against prominent Jewish people in the Chicago area is only one of scores of known incidents.) Central Intelligence Agency Director George Tenet has said that such terrorists "are expanding their networks, improving their skills and sophistication and working to stage more spectacular attacks."

Here are brief profiles, mostly taken from the year 2001 report *Patterns of Global Terrorism 2000* of the United States Department of State, Counter-Terrorism Division, and from Terrorism.com.

Al-Qaeda

Osama bin Laden's al-Qaeda group, with probably 3,000 to 5,000 members, is believed to have operations in 60 countries, with active cells in up to 30 nations, including the United States, Canada, the United Kingdom, Egypt, Libya, Pakistan, Afghanistan, Kosovo, Chechnya, Tunisia, Bangladesh, Saudi Arabia, Qatar, Yemen, Jordan, Lebanon, Algeria, Tunisia, Mauritania, Sudan, Azerbaijan, Uzbekistan, Tajikistan, Somalia, Kenya, Tanzania, Uganda, Ethiopia, Eritrea, Malaysia, the Philippines, Uruguay, Ecuador, Bosnia, and Albania.

Al-Qaeda was started in the late 1980s to unite Arabs who had fought in Afghanistan against the Soviet Union. It helped finance, recruit, and train Sunni Muslim extremists for the Afghan resistance. Its current goal is to establish a pan-Islamic caliphate throughout the world by working with allied Islamic extremist groups to overthrow regimes it sees as non-Islamic. Terrorist attacks by this group that have been foiled allegedly include blowing up the Los Angeles International Airport and blowing up scores of airplanes in the air. The Counter-Terrorism Division report states that al-Qaeda—

- "plotted to carry out terrorist operations against U.S. and Israeli tourists visiting Jordan for millennial celebrations"
- "conducted the bombings in August 1998 of the U.S. Embassies in Nairobi, Kenya, and Dar es Salaam, Tanzania, that killed at least 301 persons and injured more than 5,000 others"
- "claims to have shot down U.S. helicopters and killed U.S. servicemen in Somalia in 1993 and to have conducted three bombings that targeted U.S. troops in Aden, Yemen, in December 1992"
- "is "linked to the following plans that were not carried out"—
  —the assassination of Pope John Paul II during his visit to Manila in late 1994
  —"simultaneous bombings of the U.S. and Israeli Embassies in Manila and other Asian capitals in late 1994"
  —the "midair bombing of a dozen U.S. trans-Pacific flights in 1995"
  —the killing of President Clinton during a visit to the Philippines in early 1995
- "Continues to train, finance, and provide logistic support to terrorist groups in support of these goals" [205]

Islamic Jihad (al-Jihad)

Also known as "Egyptian Islamic Jihad" and "Jihad Group," this organization has hundreds of hard-core members. It was started in the late 1970s, and is a close partner with bin Laden's al-Qaeda, having formed an official alliance with them. Specializing in armed attacks against Egyptian government officials, it was responsible for the 1981 assassination of Egyptian President Anwar Sadat, as well as the attempted assassinations of Interior Minister Hassan al-Alfi in August 1993 and Prime Minister Atef

Sedky in November 1993. The goal is to overthrow the Egyptian government and replace it with a radical Islamic state.

Islamic Jihad has attacked U.S. and Israeli interests in Egypt and abroad, and was responsible for the Egyptian Embassy bombing in Islamabad, Pakistan, in 1995. It operates out of the Cairo area and has a network in Yemen, Afghanistan, Pakistan, Sudan, Lebanon, and the United Kingdom. The Egyptian government believes that Iran supports the *jihad* and that it obtains some of its funding through various Islamic and front organizations and through criminal activities.[206]

> They have claimed responsibility for numerous terrorist attacks against Egyptian government officials and institutions, Christian leaders and institutions, and Israeli and Western targets on Egyptian soil. Jihad recruits are trained in remote bases in Egypt, Afghanistan, Pakistan, Sudan and elsewhere....In addition they canvass local notables and institutions for donations, and collaborate with the Egyptian underworld in crime, especially against the Coptic Christian community, and may obtain some funding through various Islamic nongovernmental organizations....The Jihad group specializes in armed attacks against high-level Egyptian Government officials....[207]

HAMAS (Islamic Resistance Movement)

HAMAS began in 1987 as an expansion of the Palestinian branch of the Muslim Brotherhood, with the goal of establishing an Islamic Palestinian state that would destroy Israel. In terrorism, it is the primary rival to the Palestine Liberation Organization (PLO), and it works in secret or openly through mosques, political activity, and social-service institutions to attract members and financing, organize operations, and distribute propaganda. It has tens of thousands of supporters and has conducted scores of attacks, including large-scale suicide bombings against Israeli civilian and military targets. It "receives funding from Palestinian expatriates, Iran, and private benefactors in Saudi Arabia and other moderate Arab states." Funding is also received from supporters in the U.S. and Europe.

> By 1991, HAMAS...gained enough prestige to represent a number of Palestinian groups at a major peace conference in Tehran. Following this meeting, HAMAS split entirely with the PLO when the latter refused to accept the former's request that it be granted a significant presence on the Palestine National Council.
>
> Speculation is rampant that the group may be altering its focus from Islamic nationalism to the creation of an Islamic society....As of this writing, HAMAS, and its armed militant wing known as Iz el-Deen, carries out continued bombings (including a large number of suicide bombings), assassinations, and kidnappings of those opposed to its existence.[208]

Hizballah (Party of God)

With hundreds of hard-core members and thousands of supporters, Hizballah is "known or suspected" in numerous anti-U.S. terrorist attacks, including the suicide truck-bombing of the U.S. embassy and U.S. Marine barracks in Beirut in October 1983, and of the U.S. embassy annex in Beirut in September 1984; the kidnapping of U.S. and other Western citizens in Lebanon; attacking the Israeli Embassy in Argentina (1992); and the 1994 bombing of the Israeli cultural center in Buenos Aires.

> The group's military wing, Islamic Resistance Movement (not to be confused with HAMAS, which also uses the name), has received a steady supply of advanced explosives and detonating devices which has enabled Hizballah to create what has become their trademark: the car bomb.[209]

The Palestine Liberation Organization (PLO)

For a discussion of this group and the implication of its beliefs and activities for Islam, see Appendix D: "Are Yasser Arafat and the PLO Terrorists, and What Does This Mean for Islam?"

Terrorist Nation–States

In April 2000 the U.S. State Department designated seven nations as "state sponsors of terrorism." (Not included was Afghanistan because the U.S. did not recognize the ruling Taliban.)[210]

- *Cuba* "continued to provide safehaven to several terrorists" in 2000, including several U.S. terrorist fugitives.

- *Iran* was considered the "most active" sponsor of terrorism because of its support for militant terrorist groups in the Middle East such as HAMAS, Hizballah, and Islamic Jihad.

- *Iraq* had "planned and sponsored" terrorism in 2000, but had not attempted an anti-Western terrorist attack since its attempt to assassinate former President Bush in 1993.

- *Libya* was included for its alleged involvement in several past terrorism operations, including the 1988 downing of Pan Am flight 103 over Lockerbie, Scotland, and other incidents.

- *North Korea* "may have sold weapons" to terrorist groups such as the Moro Islamic Liberation Front in the Philippines in 2000.

- *Sudan* continues to provide a safe haven to terrorist groups, including associates of Osama bin Laden's Al-Qaeda.

- *Syria* (recently elected to the United Nations Security Council) was accused of providing safe haven to several terrorist groups, including the Popular Front for the Liberation of Palestine, and the Islamic Jihad.

ARE YASSER ARAFAT AND THE PLO TERRORISTS, AND WHAT DOES THIS MEAN FOR ISLAM?

That the question "Are they really terrorists?" has to be asked is fine testimony to the brutal efficiency with which the Palestine Liberation Organization (PLO) has marketed itself. There is "bad" terror, and then there is terror against Israel. How individuals like Yasser Arafat and groups like the PLO, Hizballah, HAMAS, and others are treated in the worldwide conflict with terrorism will offer a good indication of the resolve of the West, and of Islam itself, in regard to the future. So far, much of the world has pretty much accepted Arafat as a freedom fighter and hero, ignoring the truth and ignoring the extremely important implications of such a compromise.

The chapter "The Gaza Syndrome" in Benjamin Netanyahu's book *Fighting Terrorism* should be required reading for those concerned about dealing with terrorists. He shows how Israeli weakness in trusting an enemy who has never given any reason for trust resulted in a much greater death toll and in even worse complications. Once Israel decided to trust Arafat and withdrew from Gaza to fulfill the Oslo Accords of 1993, the only result was that Gaza become a haven for terrorists.

For a full two years after the accords were signed, Arafat did not apprehend a single terrorist, in spite of his promises. Netanyahu cites declarations in Arabic by Arafat and the PLO leadership proving that their purpose was to "talk peace and do war" with "the Zionist enemy."[211]

Noted columnist Cal Thomas points out that Arafat and the PLO have "spewed hate at the United States and bullets and bombs at Israel for decades." The Mufti of Jerusalem, appointed by Arafat, has called on Allah to destroy America. The head of the Palestine Association of Religious Scholars, Sheik Hamed Al-Bitawi, declared that "Israel and America are the source of terrorism in the world."[212]

Why Do Muslims Worldwide Support the PLO?

As far as we know, every Muslim nation on earth supports Arafat and the PLO—not one has ever repudiated them. Actions like these speak volumes. How can these nations support a war against terrorism while supporting the terror of the PLO (and having supported it for decades)? Things like this make people doubt Islam's claim to being a religion of peace. Actively supporting, encouraging, and funding terrorists who murder innocent Israeli citizens is not peaceful.

The material given below serves to illustrate the PLO's thinking and beliefs (the sermons and teachings included are only a few of the hundreds that could be cited). It also illustrates for us how Muslim religious leaders cite only the Quranic texts that promote destruction—so that they can justify and even demand unbending hatred toward non-Muslims, especially the Jewish people. That such an organization as the PLO is supported by Muslim nations worldwide gives us a strong indication of Islam's actual attitude toward terrorism.[213]

What Do Palestinian Religious Authorities Teach?

Palestinian spiritual leaders, all appointed by the Palestinian Authority (PA) political leadership, have consistently and openly taught that the current conflict between Palestinian Arabs and the Israeli Jews is part of an eternal religious war between Islam and the Jewish people. Sermons and religious instruction that are broadcast every Friday on official Palestinian TV and radio, as well as religious lessons that appear in PA newspapers and other media, show this unmistakably. Jewish people are portrayed as the permanent enemies of Allah, and the destruction of Jews is represented to be the will of Allah. "On the national level, Allah prohibits acceptance of Israel's existence and will destroy it...."

The PA religious ideology can be summarized in eight main beliefs, four about the Jews and four about Israel. In regard to the Jews—

1. Jewish people are the adversary of God (Allah).
2. Islam is engaged in a protracted religious war against the Jewish people.
3. It is a "religious obligation" to kill Jewish people.
4. The Palestinian people make up the front line in the battle against the Jews. Further, all Islamic states are duty-bound to help in this *jihad*.

In regard to the state of Israel—

1. All land between the Mediterranean Sea and the Jordan River [that is, all of Israel] is an Islamic religious trust [a *waqf*]. Indeed, any Muslim who surrenders any part of this land to Israel is fated to Hell.
2. Any accord with Israel is intrinsically impermanent, signed merely because of Israel's temporary military advantage.
3. Allah will discipline Muslim believers who evade their responsibility to war against Israel.
4. The ultimate annihilation of Israel is assured by Allah.[214]

Note the following, which is consistent with the above principles:

At least four times in recent months Palestinian religious leaders have taught publicly that the following Hadith (one of the Islamic traditions attributed to Muhammad) is authoritative for Islam today and expresses Allah's will that obedient Muslims kill Jews...: "The Day of Resurrection will not arrive until the Muslims make war against the Jews and kill them, and until a Jew hiding behind a rock and tree, and the rock and tree will say: 'Oh Muslim, Oh servant of Allah, there is a Jew behind me, come and kill him!'"(Sheikh Muhammed Abd al Hadi La'afi, responsible for Religious Teaching and Instruction in the Office of the Wakf, in the official P.A. newspaper *Al-Hayat Al-Jadida*, 18 May 2001 and 27 April 2001; Dr. Muhammed Ibrahim Madi, [speaking on] Palestinian Television in the main Friday sermons on 30 March 2001 and 13 April 2001)....[215]

Below we give more examples from the PA broadcasts. Sources emphasize that such sentiments had been expressed for a long time prior to the 2001 *intifada* (violent uprising); they also emphasize that it is likely such religious views are responsible for fueling the terror and violence that has been raging for so long in Israel.[216]

"The Jews are the Jews. There never was among them a supporter of peace. They are all liars....They are terrorists. Therefore it is necessary to slaughter them and murder them, according to the words of Allah....It is forbidden to have mercy in your hearts for the Jews in any place and in any land. Make war on them any place that you find yourself. Any place that you encounter them—kill them. Kill the Jews and those among the Americans that are like them....Have no mercy on the Jews, murder them everywhere..." (The preacher [of the foregoing was] Dr. Ahmed Yousuf Abu Halabiah, a member of the Palestinian Sharianic [Islamic religious law] Rulings Council, and Rector of Advanced Studies, the Islamic University, [as heard on] Palestinian Television, 13 October 2000).

"...Their Bible [of the Jews] today, has no light and no teachings. Their Bible today, is just a bunch of notes that were written down by people who lie about God, his prophets and his Bible.... Those who do these kinds of things are the descendants of Abelis, meaning the descendants of the satans....They fabricated a Jewish history book full of promises to Abraham, Isaac and Jacob that He will give them the land of Palestine..." (Religion class on Palestinian Television, 3 November 1998).

"All of the agreements entered into [with Israel] are temporary, until the decree comes from Allah and until the destiny from Allah is realized" (Dr. Muhammed Ibrahim Madi, Palestinian Television, 28 July 2000).

What Does Islam's Support for the PLO Tell Us?

Author and observer of the Mideast Dave Hunt points out that the deception and craft of the PLO pay big dividends to would-be terrorists.

There is a certain hypocrisy in the new outrage with which America and the world now view terrorism. History's bloodiest, most vicious and successful terrorist, Yasser Arafat, has been given the Nobel Peace Prize and embraced as a world statesman. He is proof to would-be imitators that terrorism pays big. The United Nations, European Union, and countless world political and religious leaders have sided with him in his terrorism against Israel.

Arafat and his PLO held the record for the largest hijacking (four aircraft in a single operation)—which has just been equalled—the greatest number of hostages held at one time (300), the greatest number of people shot at an airport, the largest ransom collected ($5 million paid by Lufthansa), the greatest variety of targets (40 civilian passenger aircraft, five passenger ships, 30 embassies or diplomatic ministries, plus innumerable fuel depots and factories), etc. Instead of being tried at an international tribunal as were the Nazi and Serbian leadership, Arafat's bloody exploits gained for him acceptance as a leader for peace![217]

Finally, consider this analysis given at an Israeli counter-terrorism Web site:

The post-September 11 world is a different place. In this new world, Arafat's Palestinian Authority not only belongs on the list of regimes that support terror, it is the only regime that directly engages in and justifies terror on a systematic basis....Organizations directly loyal to Arafat, such as Force 17, his hand-picked "presidential guard," and the Fatah Tanzim, have committed about half the terrorist attacks against Israelis over the past year.

The whole point of America's war against terrorism is that there are no "good terrorists." Yet the Arab world, led by the Palestinians, is trying to argue exactly that: there is terror and there is terror against Israel.[218]

Do such attitudes extend across the entire Muslim world—and to other terrorist organizations? The evidence seems to point that way. America and the West have many enemies, individually and in nation states. We trust those who want to destroy us to our own peril.

A Letter from a Friend— Do American Muslims Understand America?

I (Weldon) asked a friend with political connections what his take was on the September 11 attack. He is a member of a particularly skilled branch of the Special Forces; I reached him as he was packing to go overseas on assignment. He was kind enough to write a rather long letter, which I received about a week later. My friend asked me to try to have it published if he "didn't make it," knowing he could be killed, most likely by a Muslim radical.

"Islam is one of the world's great religions, and I learned much about it years ago through some Muslim friends who are very kind people and precious to me. But Islam was not great on September 11, when moderate Muslims who may have suspected the attack apparently said nothing of warning.

"I know most Muslims were as shocked as anyone, but something appears out of kilter here. This was illustrated on the September 30, 2001, *60 Minutes* program. Muslim leaders in America, understandably, emphasized that Islam had nothing to do with terrorism and could have nothing to do with terrorism. These individuals were undoubtedly sincere, and it is certainly true that the great majority of Muslims oppose terrorism, based on their religious beliefs.

"But were these leaders correct that true Islam had nothing to do with terrorism—never did and never could? Or, again understandably, were they being somewhat defensive, perhaps even naive about their own religion and its potential, however cleverly, to inculcate the seeds of terrorism? Are Islamic scripture, legal tradition, and history perfectly innocent? I don't think so, and I have lived in numerous Muslim cultures and studied this complex religion.

"These leaders were kind enough not to say that the U.S. had 'deserved' what happened, like some other more radical 'moderate' Muslims had said. Instead, they argued that the U.S. was an accessory of sorts to what had happened. In fact, 'bin Laden is made in the USA'—apparently meaning that American policies toward Muslim countries, Israel and Palestine, and so on, were legitimately—that is, *morally*—responsible for helping to produce someone like bin Laden. I know from a lot of personal experience that committed Muslims are dedicated first and foremost to Islam, not necessarily the country in which they live. This is one reason so many Muslims, in scores of nations, are so willing to condemn America and the West, however unjustly, in deference to Muslim interests elsewhere, as in the Middle East.

"How often I have heard that Muslim problems and grievances today go back to the Crusades, how innocent Muslims were mercilessly slaughtered by warring Christians. I wish Muslims would get their history straight—and many Americans for that matter. If I remember that history, the Crusades (1096–1291) were an attempt to retake formerly Christian Palestine. Islamic *jihad* was the cause of the Crusades. It was the success of Muslim aggression, *jihad* against Europe, that triggered Pope Urban II to call for the first Crusade in the year 1095.

"The U.S. has already been savaged today, thank you; she does not need additional help from her friends in Islamia or academia. Having suffered her worst attack in history, still in deep bereavement, I am appalled by those who would quickly blame Christians—like one minister I saw interviewed on TV—or America for what had happened.

"Here is a new idea. Why not blame the terrorists? Is that too reactionary a concept for our Marxist friends—who can't seem to let go of a carnivorous ideology that has, excuse me, been responsible for the deaths of possibly 110,000,000 innocent victims since 1917? (No outrage seen among Marxist sympathizers for that little mishap.) And that figure, I think, is given by Aleksandr Solzhenitsyn, someone who experienced the horror, wrote about it, and knows.

"Thankless people who would blame anyone or anything but those responsible apparently have little concept of personal responsibility for themselves or others. Terrorism, they claim, is the pursuit of legitimate grievances by illegitimate means. Baloney. It is deliberate murder, just as this was mass murder. Mass murderers who use charities for fundraising and teach little children to kill cannot find better comrades in hell.

"Sorry for the soapbox. One Muslim leader on *60 Minutes* stated that moderate Saudi Arabia is one of the principal supporters, worldwide, of one particular brand of fanatic Islam. (He was referring to Wahhabism, a reform Islam seeking a return to 'pure' Islam, viewing all change in Islam after the first few centuries as spurious and viewing the world in 'us' versus 'them' categories. The Taliban are cousins, I think, of the Wahhabis.) It was noted that the phrase, 'Death in the path of God is our highest aspiration,' is a view actively promoted by the Saudi regime through this particular school of Islam. Apparently, the Muslim leaders, nodding to this fact, didn't quite see how they had just set their own claim that Islam cannot be responsible for terrorism on its head, or that that particular school and radical Islam had helped birth Osama bin Laden far more than American policies. If they didn't think Wahhabism was truly Islamic, they could never prove it.

"These Islamic leaders, like so many other Muslims world-wide, warned the U.S. against pursuing Muslim terrorists in other countries too strenuously, over concern we would kill innocents and significantly increase Muslim fundamentalism and that this would lead to even more terrorism. Again, they didn't seem to understand that if such terrorism did increase, it was increasing within a distinctly Islamic religious culture. I don't know how any country, no matter how decent, can prevent innocent casualties in a war. Once attacked, viciously, self-preservation has a higher moral authority than preventing civilian casualties, though America will certainly do its best, as we did in '91 [the Gulf war]. Terrorists understand only one thing—raw power.

"Terrorists who want to destroy you *will* destroy you unless you destroy them first. Nothing justifies terrorism; if it does, anything is permitted, even the gassing of a million babies at Dachau. Nothing justifies trusting a terrorist before he's dead, unless you don't care to live. I do, I want my family to live and to be free—that's why I'm going.

"Finally, the argument was made that the Quran requires Muslims to police themselves and to rid their own ranks of something like religious terrorism. One leader even spoke of a 'jihad' against the terrorists. Wonderful, but has that been the history of Islam? Actions speak louder than words. Again, these respected leaders seemed out of touch with history. I know what is happening in the Sudan and elsewhere. In the three weeks after the September 11 terrorist mass murders, the worst in human history—acts of terror, by the way, committed by Muslim radicals citing the Quran in support—not a single Arab Muslim state had openly joined the U.S.-brokered military coalition to fully side with America against terrorism. Why? Was the massacre of insufficient proportions to generate conviction?

"Indeed, Islam seems to have done little to police itself, or to rid itself of the terrorism that had been breeding within its loins for decades and had been exported globally. (The exception was when the terrorists were trying to kill the leaders of moderate or secular Muslim states whom the terrorists considered apostate Muslims deserving of death.) To the contrary, as far as the rest of the world was concerned, Islam has more frequently looked the other way, apparently fearing the radical elements within its own borders. Ignoring evil only lets it breed. How can a world religion that stresses mercy and justice, as their holy book teaches, continue to ignore the vicious, repeated Muslim terrorism in Israel against the Jews, or far worse, genocidal slaughter in the Sudan against millions of black Christians? More than once I have wondered whether Muslims have any idea how their religion might play out if it is *not* policed.

"Thankfully, many Muslim clerics seem to have condemned the September 11 attack as 'murder.'

"Much as I respect Muslims, I guess I want to see some real action from the mullahs to deal with the terrorists, and more of 'the peace of Islam' theme before I pick up a Quran as God's Word, like my friends keep urging. As far as I can see, when one understands how evil the terrorists are, and how evil terrorism is, and its consequences in civil society, then Islamic complicity becomes all the more unjustified, indeed, abhorrent. My friends understood, but said it was not their fault. Fair enough. But it is someone's fault.

"Do I blame Islam for September 11? No; I blame Islam for permitting the climate that produced September 11. Many Muslims, including heads of state, seem torn—both with us and against us at the same time. That is something Islam must sort out. Until I see concrete evidence that moderate Muslims stand with us, wholeheartedly, in the war on terror, Muslims in America and elsewhere should not wonder when Americans like me wonder in turn about Islam or Muslim loyalties. The evil nature of the attack, the extent of the war declared, the future casualties that are sure to come, demand no less.

Hopefully, September 11 was sufficiently evil to institute some real action on the part of the Islamic world. And perhaps Israel and the West will learn to be less naive. We were warned more than once that something like this was coming.

"Bin Laden was in Saudi intelligence; he's very smart. I know his type. He knew how we would react and he already had the second through sixth waves planned with appropriate time in between for maximum effect. If we don't get his network, expect something big within six weeks. Nineteen of his people carried out September 11. If he has a thousand sleepers and we get 500 of them, do the math. He knows his success is not measured by how many he kills—it's what the constant terrorism does to a people. America will no longer be America, that's his victory. We will resist it, but we will give in to survive—that's his victory. We'll never take him alive, that's his victory. Even when we kill him there will be thousands more like him, that's his victory. The refugees and civilian casualties we get blamed for in the Muslim world, that's his victory. At some point we may be forced to threaten to use, or even use, low-yield nukes (less than 10 kilotons) against anyone who can even begin to threaten us. That, unfortunately, may be our victory.

"Our enemy has made it crystal clear, beyond any scintilla of doubt, that he will murder us and our children, and millions of other Americans, by any and all means necessary. He will take advantage of our every freedom, innocence, and lack of preparation. He will live among us and look just like us. If we don't respond immediately, with common sense, with changes in policy, and with appropriate force, then we alone are responsible for the outcome. Freedom costs dearly, and she has dangerous enemies, even within her own borders. Thank God Bush won the election; his national security team is the best in our history.

"If the American-led war on terrorism is successful, and it will be, it will be because we showed our enemies the same kindness they showed us, with fury, ruthlessly. The consequences of that outcome lie with the terrorists and those who support them, nowhere else. Muslims of good will can be tremendously helpful in this war, and hopefully they will close ranks with us.

"Regardless, people everywhere will decide if they are for America and what she stands for—or for her enemies. Americans will be watching. So will my buddies, and we can be fierce. Bin Laden and Muslim terrorists will see just how fierce we can be. We will exert a high level of violence on them, and it will be for our children's future and for those mercilessly slaughtered on September 11. September 11 was the day the gloves went off, and woe to those who don't get it. With the continued support of loyal Americans, in five or ten years we will all live in a much safer, more secure world. If I die, I die free. Please pray for us, especially when you don't see us. That will be often. But we'll be there. God bless America."

Resources List

Books and Articles

- Anthony J. Dennis, *The Rise of the Islamic Empire and the Threat to the West*.
- Ibn Warraq, *Why I Am Not a Muslim*.
- Benjamin Netanyahu, *Fighting Terrorism*.
- Craig Blomberg, *The Historical Reliability of the Gospels*.
- John Wenham, *The Goodness of God*.
- Norman Geisler, *Encyclopedia of Christian Apologetics*.
- C.S. Lewis, *Mere Christianity*.
- Abdiyah Akbar Abdul-Haqq, *Sharing Your Faith with a Muslim*.

Web Sites

- SecularIslam.org
- TheSpiritofIslam.com
- The Quran.com
- MEForum.org
- ArabicNews.com
- Terrorism.com

- Infowar.com
- SpecialOperations.com
- PotomacInstitute.org
- ApologeticsIndex.org
- The International Policy Institute for Counter-Terrorism (<http://www.ict.org.il/>).
- Answering-Islam.org
- Why Muslims Become Christians (<http://www.answering-islam.org.uk/Testimonies/>).
- Apologetics.org
- LeaderU.com (General Resources).
- Gospelcom.net (General Resources).
- Islamic Studies in Christian Perspective (<http://www.rim.org/muslim/islam.htm>).
- The Muslim-Christian Debate Web site (<http://debate.org.uk/>).

Resources Specific to the Issue of Islam and Women

Afkhami, Mahnaz, ed. *Faith and Freedom: Women's Human Rights in the Muslim World.* Syracuse, NY: Syracuse University Press, 1995.

Answering-Islam.org (<http://answering-islam.org/Women/index.html>). Various articles; detailed listing of web articles, pro and con.

Brooks, Geraldine, *Nine Parts of Desire: The Hidden World of Islamic Women.* New York: Anchor, 1996.

Goodwin, Jan, *Price of Honor: Muslim Women Lift the Veil of Silence on the Islamic World.* New York: Penguin USA, 1995.

Jabbaar, Salman Hassan. "The Place of Women in Christianity and Islam," 1994. Answering-islam.org/Women/inislam.html.

Memon, Kamran. "Wife Abuse in the Muslim Community." *Islamic Horizons* (<http://www.steppingtogether.org/article_01.html>).

Rafiqul-Haqq, M., and P. Newton. *Women in Islam.* Pioneer Book Publishing, 1994. *The Place of Women in Pure Islam.* Pioneer Book Publishing, 1996. Both available from The Berean Call Resources: <http://www.tbcorders.org/default.asp>; PO Box 7019, Bend OR 97708; 800-937-6638 or 541-382-6210.

"Wife Beating in Islam." Answering-Islam.org (<answering-islam.org/Silas/1wife-beating.htm>).

NOTES

Qurans cited:
- Maulana Muhammad Ali, *The Holy Quran: Arabic Text, English translation and Commentary* (Columbus, OH: Ahmadiyyah Anjuman Ish'at Islam, 1996)

- A. Yusuf Ali, *The Holy Quran* (Washington, D.C.: The Islamic Center, 1978)

- A.J. Arberry, *The Quran Interpreted* (New York: MacMillan, 1976)

- N.J. Dawood, *The Quran* (Baltimore: Penguin Books, 1972)

- N.J. Dawood, *The Koran with a Parallel Arabic Text* (New York: Penguin, 1997)

- Muhammad Zafrulla Khan, *The Quran* (New York: Olive Branch Press, 1997) (with Arabic text)

- J. M. Rodwell, *The Koran* (New York: Dulton, 1977).

Sura references are from the above translations. Some translations do not number either verses or paragraphs. Chapters are also numbered differently in English and Arabic.

Dialog with Muslims:

For help with this, see C.R. Marsh, *Sharing Your Faith with a Muslim* (Moody), and North Africa Mission, *Reaching Muslims Today: A Short Handbook*. Additional important materials are available from—

- Reach Out, Box 18478, Boulder, CO 80308-8478
- California Institute of Apologetics (formerly Truth Seekers), PO Box 7447, Orange, CA 92887
- Fellowship of Faith for the Muslims, 205 Yonge Street, Room 25, Toronto, Ontario M5B 1N4, Canada
- The Samuel Zwemer Institute, Box 365, Altadena, CA 91001
- North Africa Mission, 239 Fairfield Avenue, Upper Darby, PA 19082
- Africa Christian Press, 16 Morwell Street, London WCIB 3AP, England
- The U.S. Center for World Missions, 1605 Elizabeth Street, Pasadena, CA 91104.

Numbered notes:

1. <http://www.heritage.org/shorts/20010914terror.htm>.
2. Ibid.
3. <http://www.washingtonpost.com/wp-dyn/articles/A44042-2001Sep29.html>.
4. Dr. Daniel Pipes, in an interview on Chris Matthew's *Hardball*, October 19, 2001.
5. Walter R. Martin, "The Black Muslim Cult," in *The Kingdom of the Cults* (Minneapolis: Bethany, 1970 ed.), pp. 259-75.
6. J. Christy Wilson, *Introducing Islam* (New York: Friendship Press, 1965, rev.), p. 30.
7. Those by A.J. Arberry, which, in the words of Wilfred Cantwell Smith of Harvard University, is "the one that comes closest to conveying the impression made on the Muslims by the original"; that of the Iranian scholar N.J. Dawood, director of Contemporary Translation Limited and managing director of the Arabic Advertising and Publishing Company, Ltd., London, his 1997 edition being "brought as close to the original as English grammar and idiom will allow"; that of J.M. Rodwell, which "has been declared by modern scholars to be one of the best translations ever produced"; that of Muhammad Zafrulla Khan, the foreign minister of Pakistan in 1947, and President of the UN General Assembly (17th Session), which remains "strictly faithful to the text in meaning"; and that by Abdullah Yusuf Ali, *The Holy Quran*, widely used among American Muslims and considered by them among the best of translations. Indeed, "some Muslims are prepared to commend the accuracy of the best of these translations, and to admit their value as interpretation, though not official interpretation, of the meaning of the sacred text."

   While Muslims may be critical of non-Muslim translations (as, for example, Ali is of Rodwell's), one should not necessarily conclude that Muslim translations are always more accurate. For example, "Muslim translators such as Yusuf Ali will not hesitate to mistranslate the Arabic text [cf. Sura 5:76] in order to keep the English reader from discovering obvious errors in the Quran....The readers of his translation must be aware of its hidden apologetic agenda" (remarks by Robert Morey in *Islamic Invasion* [Eugene, OR: Harvest House, 1992], p.175).

8.   Morey, *Islamic Invasion*, pp. 21-23; other materials from the organizations cited in the Notes section "Dialog with Muslims." See also John Ankerberg and John Weldon, *One World: Bible Prophecy and the New World Order* (Chicago: Moody Press, 1991), pp. 110-20 and Notes.

9.   Ibid.

10.   A.M. Holt, ed., *The Cambridge History of Islam*, vol. 2 (London: Cambridge University Press, 1970), cited in Josh McDowell and John Gilchrist, *The Islam Debate* (San Bernardino, CA: Here's Life Publishers, 1983), p. 16.

11.   John Elder, *The Biblical Approach to the Muslim* (Fort Washington, PA: Worldwide Evangelization Crusade, 1978), pp. 30-31; McDowell and Gilchrist, *Debate*, p. 19 passim.

12.   See the *Wall Street Journal*'s "2001 Index of Economic Freedom."

13.   LATimes.com, September 13, 2001.

14.   Dr. Daniel Pipes, *London Daily Telegraph*, September 14, 2001.

15.   "Is Killing Jewish Women and Children Forbidden?" translated from the Arabic by Shira Gutgold, originally in the *Jerusalem Post*, September 9, 2001, quoting *Al-Watan*, Kuwait, September 1, 2001. Found at <http://www.ict.org.il/>.

16.   Cal Thomas, "Plenty of Problems to Correct," Townhall.com, September 19, 2001.

17.   This citation came from an important article, "The 'Afghan Alumni' Terrorism—Islamic Militants Against the Rest of the World," at a valuable Web site, The International Policy Institute for Counter-Terrorism, <http://www.ict.org.il/>.

18.   A. J. Arberry, *The Quran Interpreted* (New York: MacMillan, 1976), p. 15.

19.   Ibid., p. 65.

20.   Ibid., p. 140.

21.   Ibid., pp. 139-40.

22.   See our *Knowing the Truth About the Trinity* (Eugene, OR: Harvest House, 1997). Also see E. Calvin Beisner, *God in Three Persons* (Wheaton, IL: Tyndale, 1984) and Edward Bickersteth, *The Trinity* (Grand Rapids, MI: Kregel, rpt.).

23.   For example, Arberry, pp. 81, 90, 142, 178, 204.

24.   Cited in a book review in *Reach Out*, vol. 6, nos. 3 & 4, 1993, p. 15.

25.   George Houssney, "What Is Allah Like?" *Reach Out*, vol. 6, nos. 3 & 4, 1993, p. 12.

26.   For example, Sura 3:45.

27.   Arberry, p. 64.

28.   N.J. Dawood, *The Quran* (Baltimore: Penguin Books, 1972), p. 233.

29.   Ibid., p. 316.

30.   Ibid., p. 317.

31.   Ibid., p. 130.

32.   A. Yusuf Ali, *The Holy Quran* (Washington, D.C.: The Islamic Center, 1978), p. 33.

33.   Maulana Muhammad Ali, *The Holy Quran, Arabic Text, English translation and Commentary* (Columbus, OH: Ahmadiyyah Anjuman Ish'at Islam, 1996), reads "disbelieve" for "blasphemy"; and for "God is Christ", "Allah is Messiah" ("Allah is the third of three," v. 73).

34.   *Tawhid* is the doctrine of the singularity of Allah; *shirk* is its opposite, the greatest of all sins, and refers to assigning partners or companions to Allah.

35.   Arberry, p. 147.

36. Ibid., p. 75.

37. Ibid., p. 85.

38. Ibid., p. 48.

39. Ibid., p. 93.

40. Ibid., p. 220.

41. Ibid., p. 344; cf. pp. 102, 105.

42. Sura 23:104-05 in the George Sale translation (1734), as cited by Phillip H. Lochhaas, *How to Respond to Islam* (St. Louis: Concordia, 1981), p. 24.

43. Dawood, 1997, p. 85, Sura 4:48.

44. Dawood, 1997, p. 232, Sura 11:105-8.

45. Dawood, 1972, p. 372.

46. Cited in Josh McDowell and John Gilchrist, *The Islam Debate* (San Bernardino, CA: Here's Life Publishers, 1983), p. 172.

47. Arberry, p. 274.

48. Abdiyah Akbar Abdul-Haqq, *Sharing Your Faith with a Muslim* (Minneapolis: Bethany, 1980), p. 159.

49. Wilson, p. 24.

50. Arberry, p. 111.

51. Dawood, 1972, p. 255.

52. Arberry, p. 93; cf. p. 98.

53. Dawood, 1972 pp. 212-22.

54. Ibid., pp. 367-68.

55. Arberry, pp. 198-99.

56. M.M. Ali, p. 1052.

57. Musa Qutub and M. Vazir Ali, "The Glorious Quran—The Unique Divine Document for Mankind," in *The Invitation*, November 1987, vol. 4, no. 4, p. 1.

58. Arberry, p. 135.

59. Ibid., p. 229, emphasis added.

60. Morey, pp. 137-58.

61. Rodwell, p. 3.

62. Dawood, 1972, p. 253.

63. Rodwell, p. 499.

64. Arberry, p. 83.

65. N.J. Dawood, *The Koran with a Parallel Arabic Text* (New York: Penguin, 1997), p. 254.

66. Anis A. Shorrosh, *Islam Revealed: A Christian Arab's View of Islam* (Nashville: Nelson, 1988), pp. 201-19.

67. Dawood, 1972, pp. 291-92; 101:194; J.M. Rodwell, *The Koran* (New York: Dutton, 1977), pp. 473-74; Arberry, pp. 63, 83, 138, 158, 185 (cf. 258), 187-88, 190, 314, 331, 348; see also Gleason L. Archer, *A Survey of Old Testament Introduction*, rev. ed. (Chicago: Moody Press, 1985), "Appendix on Errors in Quran," pp. 506-08.

68. Don Wismer, *The Islamic Jesus: An Annotated Bibliography of Sources in English and French* (New York: Garland Publishing, 1977); cf. Arberry, pp. 242-60; Dawood, 1972, pp. 324-32, 339, 348, 285, 175-81, 319, etc.; cf. Rodwell, p. 105.

69. Arberry, pp. 135, 229.

70. Dawood, 1972, p. 365.

71. Ibid., p. 134.

72. Ibid., p. 294.

73. John Warwick Montgomery, "How Muslims Do Apologetics," in *Faith Founded on Fact: Essays and Evidential Apologetics* (New York: Nelson, 1978), p. 93.

74. For example, Khalid Jan, in his attack on biblical authority in *A Human Bible* (draft), cites such biased sources as the Jesus Seminar's *The Five Gospels* and G.A. Wells, *Who Was Jesus?* while taking other sources out of context; also see various Muslim Internet sites.

75. For an illustration, see John Weldon, "Letters to the Editor," in *The Athens* [Georgia] *Banner-Herald,* Oct. 2, 1989. See also materials from the California Institute of Apologetics and Robert Morey's "Muslims and Their Logical Fallacies," *The Truth Seeker,* Jan. 1997, as well as other debates and materials, including those resources mentioned at the beginning of this section. The interested reader should also secure literature from American Islamic societies, for example, The Islamic Center, Washington, D.C., as it relates to their treatment of Christianity.

76. Arberry, p. 85, emphasis added.

77. Ibid., p. 35.

78. Dawood, 1972, p. 384.

79. Arberry, pp. 120-21.

80. Ibid., p. 122.

81. Abdul-Haqq, pp. 22-31, 38-46, 50-53, 67-73; Arberry, pp. 185, 199, 120-22.

82. Arberry, p. 130.

83. Stephen Neill, *Christian Faith and Other Faiths,* 2nd ed. (New York: Oxford University Press, 1970), p. 64.

84. Cf. Morey, pp. 129-32, 136, and our note no. 74.

85. Norman Geisler and William Nix, *A General Introduction to the Bible* (Chicago: Moody Press, 1971); cf. F.F. Bruce, *The New Testament Documents: Are They Reliable?* (Downer's Grove, IL: InterVarsity, 1981); John Warwick Montgomery, *History and Christianity* (San Bernardino, CA: Campus Crusade for Christ, 1982).

86. Geisler and Nix, p. 375; cf. pp. 238, 267, 365-66.

87. Morey, pp. 117-20.

88. "The Origins of the Koran," SecularIslam.org.

89. Morey, pp. 120-26.

90. Rodwell, 1972, p. 1; Alfred Guillaume, *Islam* (New York: Penguin Books, 1977), p. 57.

91. William Miller, *Ten Muslims Meet Christ* (Grand Rapids, MI: Eerdmans), p. 52; Elder, p. 27.

92. Guillaume, p. 56.

93. Shorrosh, pp. 197-98.

94. "The Origins of the Koran," SecularIslam.org.

95. Dr. Rashad Khalifa, Ph.D (Masjid Tucson, United Submitters International, Tucson, AZ) <http://www.adishakti.org/al-qiyamah.htm>.

96. <http://inic.utexas.edu/menic/utaustin/course/ oilcourse/mail/turkey/0011.html>.

97. <http://www.al-qiyamah.org/www.angelfire.com/>.

98. Wilson, pp. 29-30.

99. Dawood, 1972, pp. 10-11.

100. Arberry, p. 41.

101. Dawood, 1997, p. 49.

102. Arberry, p. 46.

103. Ibid., p. 298.

104. Dawood, 1972, p. 304.

105. The Hadith is considered by many orthodox Muslims to be the authentic commentary on and explanation of the Quran. It is also viewed as a divine revelation, in which Muhammad's commandments are as binding on the Muslim as the words of Allah in the Quran. After the Quran, it is also the major source of Islamic law for individual and social behavior (Sura 53:3-4) (M. Rafiqul-Haqq, P. Newton, "The Place of Women in Pure Islam," 1996 <http://debate.domini.org/newton/womeng.html>).

106. Rafiqul-Haqq and Newton.

107. Hadith found in Sahih al-Bukhari are considered by almost all Muslim scholars to be "The most authentic" of the Hadith (Rafiqul-Haqq and Newton). Non-Muslim scholars have called into question the whole body of Hadith literature, suggesting that none of the traditions surviving can be accepted at face value. "There seems to be little doubt that practically the whole body of tradition was spurious" (Robson, "Tradition: Investigation and Classification," *The Muslim World*, vol. 1:41, p. 101).

108. Unless otherwise noted, all of the following citations in this chapter are from Rafiqul-Haqq and Newton. We strongly encourage readers to verify this information personally by reading the sources cited, as well as their sources in the Hadith. (It must also be added that Muslim apologetics in this area, as in others, sometimes leave something to be desired as to accurate treatment of sources, translating the Quran accurately, and overall candor.)

109. <http://hraic.org.uk/women_in_islam.html>.

110. "Wife beating in Islam" (<answering-islam.org/Silas/1wife-beating.htm>).

111. Hraic.org.

112. Kamran Memon, "Wife Abuse in the Muslim Community" (Islamic Horizons, <http://www.steppingtogether.org/article_01.html>).

113. <http://www.muslimnews.co.uk/paper/index.php?article=104>.

114. Bassam M. Madany, in a review of *Islam And War: A Study in Comparative Ethics* by John Kelsay (Philadelphia: Westminister John Knox Press, 1993) <http://www.safeplace.net/members/mer/mer_b010.htm>.

115. M.M. Ali, xii.

116. Ibid., p. 656.

117. <http://www.secularislam.org/wtc2.htm>.

118. Dr. Christine Schirrmacher, 1997, <http://www.visi.com/~contra_m/ab/cschirrmacher/rights.html.

119. As cited by Schirrmacher.

120. Ibid.

121. OpenDoorsUSA.org.

122. *The Voice of the Martyrs,* Special Issue; Chalcedon.edu.

123. Interview in the May 1998 *Conservative Monitor* (<http://www.conservativebookstore.com/creview/iarchive/08dennis.htm>).

124. "Is Islam Compatible With Democracy and Human Rights?" SecularIslam.org.

125. "Jihad, the Arab Conquests and the Position of Non-Muslim Subjects," SecularIslam.org.

126. Ayatullah Morteza Mutahhari, "The Holy War of Islam and Its Legitimacy in the Quran," trans. Mohammad Salman Tawhidi (Islamic Republic of Iran: Islamic Propagation Organization, 1985). (P.O. Box No. 11365/7318).

127. <SecularIslam.org/call.htm>.

128. Shaykh Sa'eed ibn 'Ali ibn Wahf al-Qahtaani, "The Levels of Jihaad," Invitation to Islam (<http://www.islaam.com/articles/objectives_of_jihaad.htm>).

129. <http://www.islaam.com/ilm/ibnta.htm>.

130. <http://home.swipnet.se/islam/articles/jehad.htm>.

131. <http://antimasons.8m.com/>.

132. Debra Friedman, Michael Hechter, "Will U.S. Be an Unwitting Tool in Bin Laden's Game?" LATimes.com, September 21, 2001.

133. *Newsweek,* January 11, 1999.

134. <http://www.nationalreview.com/buckley/buckley100201.shtml>.

135. <http://www.pbs.org/wgbh/pages/frontline/shows/binladen/who/interview.html>.

136. *Israel Today,* September 2001, p. 9.

137. Jack Kelley, "Trainees eager to join 'jihad' against America," *USA Today,* September 27, 2001.

138. Ibid.

139. Translation at ABC.com September 30, 2001 and foxnews.com, October 1, 2001.

140. Ibid.

141. *Washington Post,* October 2, 2001, Page A25; cf. v. 21: "Now tell me about your goddesses…" (Khan, 531), i.e., Arabian idols said by the pagans of Mecca to be daughters of God; see Ibn Warraq, *Why I am Not a Muslim* (Amhurst NY: Prometheus, 1995).

142. <http://www.shalomjerusalem.com/jerusalem/jerusalem42.htm>.

143. CNN interview, September 20, 2001.

144. CNN interview, October 7, 2001.

145. Dr. Jerrold Post, in Ken Ringle, "A Void Filled to the Brim with Hatred," *The Washington Post,* September 27, 2001.

146. Ken Ringle, "A Void Filled to the Brim with Hatred," *The Washington Post,* September 27, 2001.

147. October 7, 2001.

148. M.M. Ali, vi-vii.

149. Ibid., p. 1239.

150. The Sabr Foundation (P. O. Box 958, Mt. Pleasant, SC 29465-0958, USA [<http://www.islam 101.com/rights/terrorism.htm>]).

151. Reuven Paz, ICT Academic Director Specialist in Islamic Affairs, "Is There an 'Islamic Terrorism'"? September 7, 1998 (<http://www.ict.org.il/>).

152. Yossi Klein Halevi, "Islam Must Challenge Its Dark Doctrines," LATimes.com September 13, 2001.

153. "The 'Afghan Alumni' Terrorism"(<http://www.ict.org.il/>).

154. Judith Miller, "The Challenge of Radical Islam," *Foreign Affairs,* Spring 1993, in Warraq, p. 360.

155. C.J.B. le Roux and H.W. Nel, "Radical Islamic Fundamentalism in South Africa. An Exploratory Overview." *Journal for Contemporary History,* December 1998 (<http://www.duc-uz.co.za/Islam%20by%20CJB.htm>).

156. Halevi, "Islam Must Challenge Its Dark Doctrines."

157. Yoni Fighel, <http://www.ict.org.il/>.

158. Fred Siegel, <http://www.foxnews.com/story/0,2933,34586,00.html>.

159. Rob Sobhani of Georgetown University made this important comment on CNN on October 4, 2001.

160. <http://islamicity.com/articles/Articles.asp?ref=AM0109-335>.

161. <http://www.icbh.org/topics/islamter.htm> (Newark, California: September 11, 2001).

162. <http://www.themodernreligion.com/terrorism.htm>.

163. Islam.org.

164. Hasan Ziller Rahim, "Silence of the Imams," Pacific News Service, October 11, 2001.

165. *Middle East Quarterly,* June 2000 and Summer 2001.

166. See <www.danielpipes.org/cair.shtml>.

167. *TransState Islam,* Spring 1997.

168. The *Jerusalem Post,* September 20, 2001.

169. <www.DanielPipes.org/articles>.

170. <http://www.answering-islam.org/Silas/terrorism.htm#plea>.

171. Daniel Pipes, "The Western Mind of Radical Islam", *First Things,* December, 1995 (<http://www.firstthings.com/ftissues/ft9512/articles/pipes.html>).

172. David F. Forte, "Radical Islam vs. Islam" (<http://www.heritage.org/views/2001/ed091901.html>).

173. <http://www.princeton.edu/~batke/itl/denise/kharijis.htm>.

174. Ibid.

175. Forte, "Radical Islam vs. Islam."

176. <http://www.theage.com.au/news/state/2001/09/22/FFXC99DVURC.html>.

177. SecularIslam.org.

178. Maulana Muhammad Ali, *A Manual of Hadith,* 2nd ed. (Columbus, OH: Ahmediyyah Anjuman Ishaat Islam, n.d.), p. 252.

179. M.M. Ali, The Holy Quran, p. 1057.

180. Ibid., emphasis added.

181. Ibid.

182. Ali, Hadith 19:17, p. 265.

183. Ibid.

184. For example, Ayatullah Morteza Mutahhari, *JIHAD:The Holy War of Islam and Its Legiti- macy in the Quran,* tr. Mohammad Salman Tawhidi (Islamic Propagation Organization, P.O. Box No. 11365/7318, Islamic Republic of Iran, 1985), Internet copy.

185. Mutahhari.

186. Ibid.

187. "Jihad, the Arab Conquests and the Position of Non-Muslim Subjects" <http://www.secularislam.org/jihad/index.htm>.

188. Anthony J. Dennis interview, *The Conservative Monitor,* May 1998, <http://www.conservativebookstore.com/creview/iarchive/08dennis.htm>.

189. Ibid.

190. *Jihad in the West: Muslim Conquests from the 7th to the 21st Centuries,* by Paul Fregosı (New York: Prometheus Books, 1998), as reviewed by Sharon Morad, Leeds (<http://debate.org.uk/topics/books/fregosi-jihad.html>).

191. Tore Kjeilen, *Encyclopedia of the Orient* (<http://lexicorient.com/cgi-bin/ eo-direct-frame.pl?http://i-cias.com/e.o/jihad.htm>).

192. Ali, Hadith, pp. 252-53.

193. M. Amir Ali, Ph.D. The Institute of Islamic Information and Education, 4390 North Elston Avenue, Chicago, Illinois, 60641-2146, (<http://home.swipnet.se/islam/ articles/jehad.htm>).

194. "Jihad, the Arab Conquests and the Position of Non-Muslim Subjects" (<http://www.secularislam.org/jihad/index.htm>).

195. Mutahhari.

196. <http://www.islaam.com/ilm/ibnta.htm>.

197. Abdullah Azzam, at the First Conference of the Jihad, Brooklyn, New York, 1989.

198. SecularIslam.org.

199. Answering-Islam.org.

200. Ibn Warraq, p. xiii.

201. Ibn Warraq, statement about September 11, SecularIslam.org, citing E.Sivan, *Radical Islam* (New Haven, CT: Yale University Press, 1990), p. 25.

202. Ibid.

203. Ibid.

204. <http://www.terrorism.com/terrorism/Groups2.shtml>.

205. <http://web.nps.navy.mil/~library/tgp/qaida.htm>.

206. <www.Terrorism.com>.

207. <http://www.ict.org.il/>.

208. Terrorism.com.

209. Ibid.

210. Annual report, *Patterns of Global Terrorism 2000* (United States Department of State, Counter-Terrorism Division, April 30, 2001).

211. Benjamin Netanyahu, *Fighting Terrorism: How Democracies Can Defeat Domestic and International Terrorism* (New York: Farrar Straus Giroux, 1995, 1996), p. 109.

212. Cal Thomas, "U.S. Should Wage War on Radical Islam" October 19, 2000 (<http://www.reporternews.com/2000/opinion/war1019.html>).

213. Taken from "ISLAM'S MANDATORY WAR AGAINST JEWS IN PA [Palestinian Authority] RELIGIOUS TEACHING," Special Report #37, Studies on Palestinian Culture and Society (Study #4: July 2, 2001, by Itamar Marcus, Director (<http://www.shalomjerusalem.com/jerusalem/jerusalem42.htm>).

214. Ibid.

215. Ibid.

216. Ibid.

217. Dave Hunt, "A Moment for Truth," *The Berean Call* newsletter, October 2001, p. 1.

218. Ely Karmon, ICT Senior Researcher, "Are the Palestinians Considering Biological Weapons?" August 14, 2001 (<http://www.ict.org.il/>).

OTHER BOOKS BY
JOHN ANKERBERG AND JOHN WELDON